HisStory

HisStory

The Trials & Tribulations of

Henry A. Gaillard

HisStory

Copyright © 2019 by Henry A. Gaillard. All rights reserved.

No part of this publication may be reproduced, stored in a retrieval system or transmitted in any way by any means, electronic, mechanical, photocopy, recording or otherwise without the prior permission of the author except as provided by USA copyright law.

This is a work of non-fiction. Some names and identifying details have been changed to protect the privacy of individuals.

The opinions expressed by the author are not necessarily those of URLink Print and Media.

1603 Capitol Ave., Suite 310 Cheyenne, Wyoming USA 82001
1-888-980-6523 | admin@urlinkpublishing.com

URLink Print and Media is committed to excellence in the publishing industry.

Book design copyright © 2019 by URLink Print and Media. All rights reserved.

Published in the United States of America

ISBN 978-1-64367-329-5 (Paperback)
ISBN 978-1-64367-328-8 (Digital)

Non-Fiction
15.10.19

Contents

Introduction 7

Dedication 9

I. The Way it All Began… 13

II. The Army Security Agency 16

III. My First Pee Test 25

VI. Re-Entry- Back into the FIRE 30

V. Homeless 42

VI. Dealing wid da Devil 48

VII. Discrimination 51

VIII. Free At Last 55

Introduction

This relevant saga documents the Life of Henry Alston Gaillard, a proud professional Viet Nam veteran who was the recipient of one of the highest security clearances attainable while working for the prestigious Army Security Agency for sixteen years eight months before he was wrongfully discharged twice from the United States Army, attributed to the first urinalysis test for marijuana. The consequential downward turmoil his Life went through as a direct result ripped apart his existence while costing losses unimaginable. This story chronicles the Trials & Tribulations suffered by this God-Fearing Man as he weathered misery after misfortune and several near-death events with the revelations thereafter.

Dedication

This story is dedicated to the greatest Love of my Life, Bobbie Carolyn Harper, who Loved me when I could not Love myself, who supported me when I could not maintain myself. Bobbie was a friend when all I had were enemies. She helped me regain my Pride. Bobbie has given me so, so much Love that I can never ever repay her. Bobbie has been the source of **ALL** my strength through the many troubled times I encountered with my two wrongful discharges. Bobbie provided much-needed emotional support during the countless times of crisis, times when I did not know who to believe, who to trust, or what to do. Her charm never ceased to fascinate me and worked like magic to restore my self-respect. I dedicate my Life to Bobbie C. who believed in me when I could not believe in myself:

**Whenever I felt so insecure,
You built me up and made me sure.
You gave, My Pride, Back to Me!
GOD Bless You!! You Make Me Feel
BRAND NEW!!!**

18 January 2010
Henry Alston Gaillard
211 12th Street Apt 512
Columbus, Georgia 31901
706.289.2521
Henry_gaillard@hotmail.com

President Barack Obama
The White House
Washington, DC

RE: REFERENCE: FLAG UPDATE
Dear Mr. President:

I have witnessed my Constitutional Rights horrendously stripped from me and I can say that it is only my unbending Faith in God and my belief in the Office of the President, and, the United States Constitution that allows me to persevere. I Appeal to the Premier Defender of the United States Constitution.

While proudly serving on active duty in the United States Army, I aspired to continue my association with the CIA/NSA after retirement. This was abruptly ended by the wrongful results of an original urinalysis test that was tactfully used to downsize after the Viet Nam war. This test affected not only me, but many other African Americans. It just so happens that I was able to save documentation of the atrocity. I continue to endure endless troubles which are rooted with the erroneous results. The urinalysis test had a snowball effect which twisted into a vile albatross that allowed me to be dropped from accountability rolls, be busted, forced into bankruptcy, lose my family, cars, and prematurely discharged again for "Financial Instability". It even affects me today. I have been homeless for twenty (20) years. I have been thrust so deep into the depths of Depression that I am ashamed to let my four (4) grandchildren see me as a dismal failure. Each and every sleepless night since, I relive the madness that has horrifically ripped apart my existence and constantly ask myself what I have done to deserve this treatment!?

I am living proof that discrimination is alive and well in this country. Yes, we have an African American President, and many African Americans holding positions of prominence and authority in and out of the government. This does very little to distinguish the overt discrimination that utilizes an elaborate, convoluted well-disguised sinister plan to keep hateful beliefs alive and well. Examples of this are the plentiful slips of tongues that hateful whites exhibit, and then attempt to cover-up with, "oops, I'm sorry!"

In the midst of this madness, I sought federal employment to gain my retirement posture. I was faced with discrimination so severe that I was forced to file a Hostile Workplace discrimination complaint. I was discriminated because I was homeless and physically disabled. The irony is that the same agency that actually caused me to be homeless and physically disabled had the audacity to discriminate against me. When I brought this into the mixture, I faced problems beyond comprehension. Early into this, I implored the District Court to appoint me an attorney. It seemed logical since Department of Army saw fit to appoint one to me when they realized their mistake with the urinalysis test and wanted to get me back onto active duty wherein I could be officially ruined. I begged, pleaded with almost every attorney in this area. Maybe it was my color, my economic status, or my southern, low-land, 'Gee-Chee' dialect that failed to get me appropriate representation. When the statute of limitations drew near, I decided to file the lawsuit, Pro Se. The case has not seen true justice.

Example:

This case was filed before the case of CPT Connie Rhodes, the white blond female officer that did not want to deploy so she questioned the President's birth. She even got three-inch headlines in the local newspaper. My case went before the same Judge Clay Land, and while he kicked her case out of the court as 'frivolous', he forwarded my case to another district, Montgomery, Alabama. I have even had professional journalists inform me that the stories that appeal to the public are stories involving either blond white women or gay folk. My appeal to you, Mr. President, is to have a member of your staff review this packet and inform me how could the 11th Circuit Court of Appeals arrive at such a questionable decision. I also have concern because when I completed the application, and, sent my $450.00 for Appeal, I specifically made note that I desired to appear before the court. This did not happen. They **Affirmed** that I had not exhausted Administrative Remedies. Attributed to the concerted style of discrimination utilized by the Cemetery Director, it took me, while homeless, sometime to grasp exactly what was going on. At all times I remained within legal parameters. If this decision was made for the greater good, the greater good should not be to emasculate a Proud Black Man in such a despicable, hateful, way.

Please forgive me for distracting you with this personal problem of mine. The Leadership you display is indeed working to make this country stronger than it ever has been. <u>I Pray that you may understand that there is no other person to turn to regarding this.</u>

**RESPECTFULLY,
HENRY A. GAILLARD**

I. The Way it All Began…

Attributed to severe head trauma sustained in a tragic automobile accident during 1978, I have been diagnosed with Organic Brain Syndrome with pre-dementia. The frightening prognosis is that I will eventually lose my ability to remember events. That was only the first severe trauma to my brain. I remained confined to Walter Reed military hospital in Washington, DC for 89 days suffering from amnesia. One amazing fact about that was that even though I had a severe concussion with loss of memory, even before Department of Army did, I **STILL** managed to call my Mama in Charleston, SC; **COLLECT!** When she answered, I simply said, "Mama, I'm alright', and hung up the phone. My Loving Mama, probably thinking I was somewhere drunk, had the presence of mind to call the Operator to find where the call was originated. When the Operator told her Walter Reed Hospital, my Mama had her **FIRST** airplane ride in her **LIFE!!** When my Mama arrived the prognosis from the Doctors was that I was never going to be the same again. **But, here comes GOD.**

I remained in Walter Reed for 89 days. The bulk of my hospitalization was spent behind locked doors in the Mental Ward. After thirty days, I was granted more privileges. After eighty days, my Psychiatrist, Dr. War, came to me and said that he was going to get me a weekend day-pass wherein I would be able to walk the streets of Washington, DC. In my present state of mind, I did not fully comprehend the doctor's intentions. One fact that those mind doctors were serious about; **INDOCTRINATION.** He wanted to see if I was inculcated enuff to be a part of society. Well, I did not think on that level, soooooo I let the six (6) paychecks remain in the hospital safe and commenced to playing pool throughout the entire weekend. Monday morning, I was **FIRST** to see Dr. War. "Henry, looks like you have serious fear about returning to society!!" **WHAT??!!** I merely wanted to save my money until I was discharged cas' Washington is a **COSTLY** city. Soooo, after convincing the doctor of this, I prepared to walk through the streets of Washington the next weekend. And walk I did… Since my Loving Mother told Dr. War that I'd been a **HEAVY** drinker since the breakup of my marriage,(evidently she forgot I was in Turkey…) I sat in 'Naked Girlie' bars(12 months abstinence) drinking orange juice because I **KNEW** that I would be given a pee test when I returned.

After I passed a battery of mental tests from my Psychiatrists, I was allowed to return to active duty after thirty days convalescent leave. In 1999, when I was out of the army, I was in another near-death horrific accident which blinded me in my left eye. Therefore, I am compelled to document my story. I am a casualty of one of the first urinalysis tests administered by the United States Army at Fort Sill, Oklahoma during 1984. Because of the difficulties suffered by me, and the resourceful ways that I discovered to deal with them, the army has drastically changed the way they manage pee tests. Nonetheless, through it all I have recognized that all things are relative. Each and every encounter I experienced in my Life, good and bad, combined, have brought me to the stance I control today. The secret was that I found methods which enabled me to endure the bad and exploit them to become edification to generate usefulness. This is not just yak. It took extraordinary vision, unyielding Faith in God, and consistent Prayer to weather the drawbacks. And, there have been pitfalls! Yes; Prayer works. That is why I Thank God for all that has happened to me; every loss, all the devastations, injuries, and forfeitures. If it had not been for all of those, I would not be where I am today. … it could have been a whole lot worse.

I readily recall when I was three years old acting as a rambunctious lad on Cooper Street, I was playing leap frog on my folded-up wooden high chair that was in the room. I badly ruptured myself. The doctor told my parents that it was doubtful that I would ever father a child. But, the doctor does not know what GOD do. Tiki was a child born out of my Love for her Mother. I truly did not really want to go to college. I felt that college was not the only way to succeed in Life. Soooo, when Pamela got pregnant, I used that as the excuse to leave school. Yet, while I felt justified with my reasoning to walk away from education, this shattered the dreams my Mother held for me. She just **KNEW** I was going to be a next Black Attorney. I saw my Mother weep as I had never seen her cry before.

After leaving college, I labored delivering **HEAVY** furniture to support my new young family. Every day my Mother would beg me to do something worthwhile with my Life. **GOD** fixed it so my place of employment was directly across from the federal building in Charleston. One day during lunch I went to the army recruiter. When I took the entrance examination, my score was high enough that I was selected to work for the prestigious **Army Security Agency.**

I did not fully understand all the ramifications surrounding working for the elite ASA. I was never able to be the Father I wanted to be to Tiki because her Mother filed for divorce while I was stationed with the ASA in Turkey. You see, throughout my Life I was **NEVER** one to question GOD. My Mama used to **ALWAYS** say, **"God ain't gonna put more than you can handle."** That's probably why I was able to manage all of the obstacles, because when I was born, delivered by a mid-wife in a ramshackle house at 69 Cooper Street, Charleston, South Carolina, I weighed 11 pounds 8 ounces. My older sister was born on January 1st, and my older brother was born on December 29th, OF THE ME YEAR!!! I truly Thank GOD that condoms were not too popular back then… Now, sentimentally I sleep in the very same bed I was born in; probably conceived in, **TOO!!!** I was a real challenge for my Mother, and, as I was growing up, each and every time when my Mother would beat/punish me, she would remind me of the torment I'd put her through. Sooooooo, quite naturally I developed some convincing conversational skills to avert, or at least lessen the punishment.

My Mother had this dear friend, Miss Vi, and she and my Mother would talk every day. Rain or shine, they would speak to each other on the old-skool black telephone. Earlier I had noticed that Miss Vi **ALWAYS** would make my Mama laugh when they would converse. Many times Miss Vi would have my Mother cackling so hard that any punishment I was about to get was not as rough as it would have been without the laughter. Soooo, now that my Mother has passed, each year in her memory I send a Mother's Day card to Miss Vi, cas' she literally saved my Life many, many times! We called Miss Vi Miss Vi since we were kids. She and her husband, Mr. Benjamin Coakley had been married for many years, but, we children only knew her as Miss Vi. Nowadays, all three of us are well beyond fifty years of age, but we still call her Miss Vi.

xxxxxxxxxxxxxxxxxxxxxxxxxxxxxxxxxxxxxxxxxxxxxxxxxxxxxxxxxx

II. The Army Security Agency

During 1977, Five of us left the 313th ASA Battalion of Fort Bragg, NC headed to Detachment 4, Sinop Turkey. This was atributed to the increasing friction between Greece and Turkey over Cyprus. The Greeks were upset because Turkey had invaded Cyprus during 1974, and with United States supplied weaponry, and against United Nations authority, was slaughtering the Greeks on the island of Cyprus. This initiated the suspension of U.S. aid to Turkey, our nations' greatest partner in the region. Turkey in return closed the twenty-six (26) U.S. bases in the country. Two of the bases were Top Secret. Detachment Four, Sinop was one of the two.

United States did not readily want to turn over control of all of the highly classified signal monitoring equipment to the Turks, so this dictated that a skeleton crew would be dispatched to 'baby-sit' the equipment for the duration. We all met at John F. Kennedy Airport to fly to Turkey. We flew from New York to Rome. We got to Rome immediately after Red Army Terrorists had bombed the airport. Security was extremely tight; we **STOOD** inside a glass partition surrounded by armed guards with machine guns for one hour while the plane was re-fueled for the flight to Istanbul, Turkey. We arrived in Istanbul at 0900 in the morning. There was too much snow for the flight so we boarded buses for an eighteen hour bus ride to Ankara.

Ankara truly reminded me of a high-rise 'Bedrock', (Flintstones) because the Turks did not use concrete too professionally. Anyway the Pan American representative who rode with us left us on a downtown street-corner 0500 in the morning. Now, none us spoke any Turkish which only made this situation that much more troublesome. Anyway, out of the 'blue' came this Air Force Captain and he directed us to a Transient House for American personnel. When we got there, the unit which was atop one of the highest mountains in the country advised us to not retain rooms because they were sending a flight to pick us up. Soooo, we meandered around the hotel, amazed at the sights and sounds of this primitive country.

The flight picked us up at around 1100 that morning and we got to the mountaintop about two hours later. We were all trained telecommunications personnel and our security clearance status was clearly established so we were directed to immediately man the TeleCommunications Center. A message came in with 'Flash' precedence stating that exactly twenty minutes after we left the hotel it was bombed to smithereens. This let us know just what to expect for 364 more days!! Now, it was too early to get Travel Pay soooooo we pooled our remaining travel funds together and together the five of us had only $3.23. We went to the Class VI (Liquor) store and there we purchased a gallon of bourbon for $3.10. Yes, we drank excessively while in Turkey. If we had no food, we **AlWAYS** had booze!

Our only job was to 'baby-sit' the Top Secret reconnaissance equipment that the United States did not want the Turks to get their hands on. One **REAL** worry in Turkey was everyday seeing the twenty-five evacuation containers for dead bodies which were stacked directly across from our barracks! And, to have just barely survived the hotel bombing in Ankara truly paved the way for us to become habitual drunkards! Turkey was a isolated, hardship Top Secret assignment atop a mountain, and Turkey has some **HUGE** mountains. I really did not understand enough about the secretive duty to fully explain things to my wife. Army Security Agency regulations dictated that to preclude the possibility for blackmail, full disclosures were required pertaining to any awkward situations to include sexually transmittable diseases, STDs. Turkey was a very dirty country. I was there five days and contracted 'crabs' from a wool blanket that was brought out of dusty storage. And, these were some colossal **CRABS**. I was quite naïve regarding louse. Since we were a skeleton crew, we each had a six-man room to ourselves and I was lying in bed naked reading and drinking wine. I felt an itch so I reached under the blanket and scratched. I went back to read. I immediately had to scratch again. Then I lifted the grimy blanket, and saw hundreds of lice about the size of small roaches swarming over my testicles. Terrified, I ran to the shower since the clinic only opened at 0730 daily. Since this was 2200 hours, I took 73 showers that night, one approximately every seven minutes. I stood in front of the clinic at 0715, itching, and waiting in torment. The nosy blonde female medical clerk who signed me in did not want to leave the question blank why I wanted to see the Doctor and persistently questioned me. So, I leaned in about two inches from her and said, "I have the crabs!!" She leaped back! Once inside, the medical personnel claimed that I probably had been with the Gypsies who frequented the surrounding woods. After I attempted to assure them that I had only just arrived, and was ignorant of anything, the doctor gave me the louse cream to wash with; I had never, ever, **EVER** experienced such a feeling of bliss!!

Nevertheless, Arlington Hall Station, ASA headquarters in Washington, D.C. sent a letter to my wife informing her that I had contracted a STD, with no mention of the moldy, infested blanket. Because we were an isolated assignment, mail was haphazard, and this was really bad during winter months; maybe twice a month, so I was truly unable to defend myself from any accusations. Since I was a young soldier, SGT/E-5, ignorant to the unique Army Security Agency regulations, I didn't even know the disclosure letter was mailed.

When I returned after eleven months I saw the letter and my wife who was a virgin when I met her was two months pregnant. She had already filed for divorce. She moved with my beloved daughter to Florida while I was stationed in Virginia and we lost contact with each other. We have since restored contact, yet, I really regret the years with her that I was not there to do the things a Father should do with his daughter. Tiki is always in my heart, and she remains foremost in my Prayers & thoughts. She will always be my only Baby.

Turkey was a civilization with its own way of dealing with situations. And you best believe me, these were some wicked ways! Take the Turkish Taxicabs. Because we were at an isolated site in the mountains, we were not allowed to drive. At the newcomers briefing we were strongly advised that if we are in a Turkish Taxicab and he has a wreck; **KICK** open the door and **RUN** because Turkish law dictates that the driver would not have had the collision if he were not hired by you. And, after the hellacious scare with the parasites, it did not surprise me to learn that there was a serious contagious sexually transmittable disease in Turkey **LONG** before AIDS!! This character attacked the genital area and resembled 'blooming flowers', hence the name, 'Roses'. The Gypsies were notorious with this malady! Since there was no known cure, I did not need sex **THAT** bad! Then there's the Turkish money, the Lira. All Turkish currency has the picture of Kemal Attaturk, the Father of modern day Turkey. If you see a bill on the ground and you try to conceal it by placing your feet on it, that is a National Crime, and, you seriously do not was to go to jail in Turkey!!! There was a contingency of British forces along with a battalion of Turkish troops assigned. One thing I learned quite, quite well. You cannot out drink Brit!!! They threw parties every Thursday, and, to get admitted you would have to down a glass of Whiskey at the door!!

Turkish troops also manned the gates to the Operational Compound, yet they did not have the combinations to the secure areas. Our only operational work done consisted of transmitting/receiving messages since the base was 'officially' closed. I recall during the cold, cold winter months when it would snow soooo hard that the snow would become eight-foot snowdrifts, and, we would have to install a rope between the barracks and the Operational Compound so as to travel to work. Detachment 4 had enormous antennas located around the fenced-in Operational, OPS. Building and there was a large field where specified large antennas were situated. One day when I was manning the TeleCommunications Center where I held the position as Trick Chief, apparently the bearings on the motor of one of the large antennas adjacent to the Ops building malfunctioned and permitted the antenna to rotate, similar to the way it would react when operational. I was unaware of this until a Turkish Colonel along with six armed Turkish guards appeared at the Vault Door 'peep-hole', a small opening located at eye-level that confirmed the identity of anyone requesting entry. This Officer demanded to enter to verify that operational work was being done which would have been in violation of the accord made between the two countries, U.S. and Turkey. I did not open the door, but I quickly recalled the contingency plans to destroy the classified equipment if the door was breached. All the classified cryptographic equipment was situated within eight seven-foot steel racks. Atop the racks were 'Thermite Grenades' which had the ability to become sooooooo hot that the entire rack would melt within thirty (30) seconds. Also, I was able to tell this Turkish Colonel 'No' because the Vault Door was reinforced steel, twelve-inches thick and would have deflected any bullets if fired upon. Well, the base U.S. Commander soon arrived and was able to placate the Turkish Colonel, but, the Turkish Colonel definitely wanted to get me thrown out of the country for disobeying him!! **BOY**, how I wish that was able to have been done!!

Troops in Turkey previously had Diplomatic Immunity. Because of the vast difference in national laws/statutes, this protected the gregarious-minded Americans. And some American soldiers had been known to exploit the **PRIVILEDGE** of having Diplomatic Immunity. Turkish women are known to be somewhat gullible when it comes to dealing with an American. Shrewd soldiers have been known to use this naïve way to their advantage. This exploitation was done so frequently that Turkey only would allow U.S. troops in-country, and each of us had to be personally invited by Turkey to be assigned within the country, if we could be prosecuted under Turkish Laws. And, you **DO NOT** want to go to jail in Turkey!! Turkish prisoners are fed by their respective families. This meant that any American imprisoned in Turkey would have to be fed by the American military. For Christmas that year, a whole Turkey was sent to the prison for the four (4) Americans confined. By the time the turkey reached its destination, after it had passed through sooo many 'hungry' hand, there was only enuff for a couple of sandwiches.

Six months later, we had a 'Half-Way' party signifying that half of the 12 month tour was completed. This was just anuther (hic) reason to get drunk. We were so isolated, we could not get a USO Tour Show to come to us, so a few of us who had some musical skills located a set of drums, a Bass Guitar, a Piano, and I played the Tenor Saxophone. The **ONLY** song that we were able to 'master' was "Chameleon", by Herbie Hancock. This song was originally over fifteen minutes long, but we four guys played this song, repeatedly, **ALL** night!! Everybody was dancing, drinking, and happy, singing, dancing, drinking, and happy…!!

Attributed to some rare extenuating circumstances, I was allowed to leave this assignment after eleven months. This entailed that I had to ride a civilian bus filled with Turkish civilians on a eight-hour ride down the mountain. THIS WAS A FEAT IN ITSELF!! First, the primary method of travel in this section of the country was a wagon pulled by either a goat or ox. Soooo, when these folk would ride on a speeding bus, motion sickness was rampant. Then in Turkey, as I found out, woman and children ride in the front of the bus while men ride in the rear. This people take animals on the bus with them!! I am talking about chickens and goats. Well, when I saw this, I sat in the seat just opposite the driver. This action caused several of the men to quickly attempt to get me to understand that I was in the wrong location. I am thinking that in this country, a Black Man **STILL** has to be relegated to the rear!!?? Then one guy explained the situation to me broken English, so, I went to the seat in the extreme rear of the vehicle so as to stick my head out the window 'cas smoking was indeed allowed on the bus, and, that combined with the smell of chickens, goats, and unwashed humans was toooo much to take. There was this usher going back and forth down the aisle passing out plastic baggies and hand solution. I found out what this was about… Turks were not used to riding, speeding down winding roads along the mountain. Most get upset stomachs. The usher would give the riders the plastic baggies to puke in and then he would throw it out of the windows. I learned of this directly as I had me head sticking as far as possible out of the rear window when I split-second evaded a bag of green puke that was about to smash into my head. **WHEW!!** That was **ONE** memorable ride!!!

I managed to leave Detachment 4, Sinop Turkey and was assigned to 307nd Army Security Agency Battalion at Vint Hill Farms Station in Warrenton, Virginia, 25 miles outside of Washington, DC. In 1978 I was in a horrific accident outside Washington, DC while stationed with the 307th ASA Battalion, Vint Hill Farms Station, and Virginia. I was a passenger, asleep, in a car driven by a friend as he ran a stop sign into a four-lane highway where he was struck by four cars and a tractor-trailer. Walter Reed was the second hospital I was taken to after the accident, and when I regained consciousness and started to walk out of the hospital without authorization continuously, I was placed in the Psychiatric Unit where I remained for 89 days, being treated for a severe concussion/amnesia. After my hospitalization, and after my convalescent leave, I went back onto active duty at Vint Hill Farms Station, Virginia, "the best kept secret of the army!!"

Vint Hill also had an immense antenna field. One mission at Vint Hill was to monitor Latin America. Duty at Vint Hill was very, very sweet. Duty was so laid-back that when my unit would go to the field, the NCO Club would close for the duration. Throughout my military service, I was fortunate to have been assigned to several challenging, demanding positions. The United States Army Security Agency (ASA) was the United States Army's signal intelligence branch. ASA was under the operational command of the Director of the National Security Agency (DIRNSA) located at Fort Meade, Maryland; but had its own tactical commander at Headquarters, ASA, Arlington Hall Station, Virginia.

Besides intelligence gathering, ASA had responsibility for the security of Army communications and for the electronic countermeasures operations. In 1977, the ASA was merged with the US Army's Military Intelligence component to create the United States Army Intelligence and Security Command (INSCOM).

My task was to provide satisfactory telecommunications support to all authorized Critical Communications Users. Before the advent of the Personal Computer, authorized users who wanted to communicate with others at a distance were required to present a hard copy of the message to a central Telecommunications Center where the highly trained operators used the most advanced electronic and cryptographic equipment to prepare and secure the message in its proper format for transmission. I operated completely under the direction of the National Security Agency.

The TeleCommcenters were designated Special Security Operations Facilities, and each and every message sent or received dealt directly with national security. Within Special Security Operations, timeliness was crucial. Messages were assigned different classifications and precedence's by an originator. All gathered information had time-sensitive value depending on its importance and classification, Information was passed through intelligence channels within hours of intercept for the lowest-priority items, but in as little as 10 minutes for the most highly critical information. Understand that means ten minutes from time of receipt by the servicing SSO to receipt by the addressee.

I can recall many times stationed overseas where we would be working shift work and we would not be advised that a General Officer was in the area. Ignorance did not preclude responsibility. Be advised that all Special Security Operations are affected by any and all events worldwide. Rising through the ranks, I was able to obtain the position of Team Chief in 1982 while at my most dynamic assignment, 302nd Army Security Agency Battalion, SSO V Corps.

The Team Chief position was an authorized E-7 slot. My grade was E-6. In this position, I managed four telecommunications center shifts, consisting of at least five (5) members, each. Since we were located downtown Frankfurt, Germany, we might of just as well had been assigned to 'New York City'!! Just like New York, Frankfurt is a 24 hour city with entertainment all day, all night, and, to have dependable, reliable operators on a consistent basis was a task in itself. Because our mission was classified, the majority of persons assigned to the CommCenter were people not wanted at the Motor Pool, where all vehicles are maintained. So, we had an abundance of female operators. A **REAL** challenge was to have to work walking distance from the bustling nightlife in Frankfurt and get the young workers, male and female to come to work!! I made it possible for them to live on the Economy, downtown, wherein they were away from the barracks humdrum, details, etc. But to ensure they would come when beckoned, there was always the realization that if they did not perform satisfactory, they would be assigned to the Motor Pool. It worked!!

Yet, once terrorism began to take hold of society, we experienced, first-hand, bombings intended to frighten the Americans in Frankfurt. We worked in a large old German building that was designated as V Corps Headquarters. Our SSO Operations Center was in the basement. Access to the building was very easy since we were downtown Frankfurt. One quiet night, some terrorists decided to damage the headquarters building, so they placed a large bomb adjacent to the Officer's Club which was directly behind the main building. The damage done was substantial!! Next, the same group started placing bombs beneath the cars of American civilians. Since my family lived in Government that was located on the economy, this really got my attention, sooooo I started parking in the General Officers parking spots which were directly in front of the building and very, very close to the Military Police who guarded the building. We worked shift work. This means we entered this building at all times during a 24 hour period. Heck, there were eight spots for the Generals, and I happened to be the only Non-Commissioned-Officer who had an automobile and I was definitely not going to be maimed by some wayward terrorist bomb!!

Several American owned cars were severely damaged with bombs placed under the car. Eventually, I was banned from parking on the Abrams Building complex because I used unauthorized parking spaces! I then started parking on the street 1000 feet away. It was there on the fourth night that terrorist(s) placed a bomb that devastated my beautiful 1978 Chrysler LeBaron. I **HAD ONLY JUST ENTERED THE BUILDING FIFTEEN MINUTES EARLIER!!!** These lunatics continued with this form of terror until they actually placed another bomb on the Abrams complex that really got the United States attention. Unbeknownst to them, it actually was the Special Security Office Operations air conditioner that sustained the damage. And, an attack on one SSO is an attack on ALL SSOs worldwide.

We were responsible for passing/receiving critical intelligence message traffic on a reliable basis, so, we had to have the most dependable operators. To achieve this, I provided personnel assigned to the SSO ComCenter with the best possible assignment perks. I was allowed to obtain 'Separate Rations', money for food, for my personnel. We operated on different shifts and this meant that all personnel would not be available for the meals at the times when they were provided. We also worked twelve-hour shifts. This made possible the implementation of Skill-Qualification-Training, SQT, for the different job positions utilized within the Telecommunications Center. Under my management, SQT scores were increased by an average of 40%. Being assigned to Frankfurt had its share of perks.

One bonus was that it was the 'Gateway' to Europe which meant that this was the site where Port Calls terminated/originated. Charleston, South Carolina is also a Port Call site. Several times a year I would take a flight back to Charleston. This flight was done on a "Space Available' basis. Airlines want their planes to fly 100% capacity. If there is a seat available, that is the seat that would be afforded me. At times it was even a 1st Class seat. Travelling the eight hours back was somewhat hectic because Charleston was ALWAYS packed with outgoing troops. I discovered that flights out of Dover, Delaware were made five (5) times daily. The first time I went there, I was 295 on the list. Mostly C-5s fly out of Dover, and each plane has seat above the cargo area towards the tail for 100 personnel. There were eight flights out of Dover, so being number 295 meant that I would be leaving out within two (2) hours!!

Another bonus was that since I held a Top Secret clearance, I was always designated the courier for the flight. As courier, I had the responsibility for ensuring that the container(s) are loaded onto the flight. The courier is the last to get on the plane and the first to get off. Also, I was also able to act on a serious concern I had questioned several times since being assigned. The SSO produced thousands of pages of highly classified waste, daily. SSO destruction of classified waste was a weekly event that consisted of two operators to carry the waste, and, two Military Policemen to provide security for this highly classified waste. My concern was that the destruction facility used an incinerator. Added to that, the incinerator was a distance away from the SSO. Local nationals manned the facility. As 95% of message traffic passed through our channels restricted foreign dissemination, this had the potential to be a serious compromise. Also, physical sifting of the debris was severely limited.

My suggestion, which was passed to the Lieutenant General, V Corps Commander, was that the SSO procure a Disintegrator. A Disintegrator is capable of destroying all traffic produced by the facility, and, it is able to destroy on-site. For obvious reasons, I was reluctant to pass this suggestion through the popular Army Suggestion Program. The V Corps Commander was impressed with my suggestion and within 60 days, a Disintegrator was on-site. Although I received a monetary award, I wish to reiterate that my first and foremost interest was national security.

The SSO Telecommunications Center was required to be operational 24 hours daily, seven days a week. All of our customers were either directly involved with Military Intelligence or Military Counterintelligence. We also had the distinct privilege to provide input on a consistent basis to the President's Daily Intelligence Briefing. As Telecommunications Station Chief, I was constantly challenged to analyze different operational facts and data to fulfill the constantly changing mission.

I was tasked with providing a weekly briefing to the V Corps Commander. I was commended for my oral attributes. My presentations were constantly concise, clear and accurate. As Station Chief, I was required at different times to facilitate communications from unique covert sources. As required by regulations, I was the custodian for several months keying material for each circuit that terminated at our center. The keying material is what was required to allow the individual cryptographic equipment to properly encrypt/decrypt message traffic. We terminated ten(10) circuits. As our mission was always 'LIVE', the ability to make the right decisions, sometimes split- second decisions, was even more prevalent. I remain constrained by the signed NDA, Non-Disclosure Agreement.

I can proudly say that under my direction, 302nd ASA Special Security CommCenter was always able to maintain its well-deserved motto, the "Best of the Best". Throughout my tenure, I NEVER went to any of the famed Training Sites. The only time we had to go to the field was when the General went to the field, and, if the General stayed in a castle, we stayed the same castle, because we provided him with direct access to his personal telecommunications, called 'BackChannel'. This was a form of communications where the bulk had 'Handling Instructions' labeled 'Eyes Only'. Even though there was hard copy provided, maybe designating it as "Eyes Only' made them disavow able.

I remained in Frankfurt close to seven years. The way I saw it, the quicker I left, the quicker I would have to return, and, the **NEXT** assignment may not be as beautiful as this one. Compared to the rest of Germany, Frankfurt was **PARADISE!!** Each year Arlington Hall Station and National Security Agency required personnel in my Grade/Position were priority requirements for the 302nd ASA Bn. They paid me an extra $125.00 a month for each month I extended. That was combined with the $75.00 a month I received for overseas pay. Heck that was an extra $200.00. But, after the start of the seventh year, somebody saw the security regulation that stated that persons with the security classification, Top Secret Special Intelligence Category IV was only allowed to be out of the continental United States five (5) years at a time. I was given thirty days to leave the country.

At that time we were allowed to choose the next assignment by picking it from a computer. When I entered my rank and MOS, the three choices that came up for me was two on Fort Hood, Texas, and one at Fort Sill, Oklahoma. Well, I never ever wanted to go to Fort Hood, so I chose Fort Sill. At first, duty at Fort Sill was not that bad. I was an Instructor at the United States Field Artillery School, and additionally held the position as COMSEC Custodian. As COMSEC Custodian, I was the sole person responsible, by hand-receipt for EVERY piece of cryptographic equipment assigned to Fort Sill, Oklahoma.

We lived in an eleven-room house on a corner in downtown Lawton. My then wife secured a job at a bank. As she had worked in American Express bank in Frankfurt, Germany, this was seemingly a natural progression. She really loved that position. Shortly thereafter, her Mother went to an appointment at Cobb Hospital in Phenix City Alabama to get treatment. Part of the medical care involved the insertion of dye into her system so as to be highlighted via x-ray. Her Mother had a immediate react ion to the dye and lapsed into a comma. When my wife was informed, she went directly to Phenix City.

III. My First Pee Test

The dubious way the test was conducted was that the subject, me, provided a sample, and it was "secured", then 'couriered' across the country to North Carolina to the private contracted laboratory, CompuChem. It took one month for the results to be returned. Many soldiers were detrimentally marked by this process. The greater majority of those 'identified' were Black soldiers. During that period, those in power in Washington made the decision to downsize after the Viet Nam war.

While researching this situation, a knowledgeable person brought to my attention that after all wars there is a downsizing done. With that thought in my mind, I still feel that it was ugly the way that urinalysis tests were being utilized to reach quotas. Commanders were given specific quotas to achieve the goal. So, the newly acquired urinalysis test was one of the techniques blatantly, but successfully used. Units would have a company-wide test, and, when the results came back over thirty days later, those 'targeted' soldiers, mostly Black, were given the results and without question or dispute have their lives & careers ruined.

The situation was so disparate that several members of various units felt that there had to be an underlying condition such as the melanin in the Black skin or the poppy seeds we ate so readily with hamburger buns. Some even assumed that eating Collard Greens made the samples go positive! To further establish credibility with this farce, Fort Sill told soldiers if they were able to provide a reliable polygraph the results would be discarded. Now, polygraphs are truly judgmental. That is probably why results from polygraph tests are not admissible in a trial. It could be it is the process of attaching all those intimidating wires to your body or the relevant recollections the subject may have/had that tends to allow the examiner to emphatically state that deception exists. Many, many incorrect positive urinalysis tests were given so that the army could arrive at its desired goal. **Later, I was given a letter, which originated with the U.S. Army Trial Defense Service which stated that, "under the stress caused by fear of detection, a person may experience certain autonomic responses. Polygraph examinations may be questioned either by doubting the scientific premise of the testing procedure itself, or by doubting the proficiency of the examiner." It went on to conclude that, "it is the intimidating appearance of the equipment that elicits 'confessions' by subjects being compelled to give a 'post test statement. For, unlike the results of the polygraph examination, the 'post-test statement' is admissible in court. There is a great deal of difference between accepting the idea that "lie detector tests" are good tools for getting admissions and accepting the idea that the technique is in fact an accurate method for distinguishing the liar from the honest man". Three physiological** responses are measured by the polygraph device: blood pressure/pulse, breathing and galvanic (electrical) skin resistance. The machine does not directly measure anything else; it is the examiner who, on the basis of the responses, infers deception. But the practical difficulty with this process is that there is no set of responses that is uniquely – or even distinctively – the product of lying. The fear of deception itself does not produce a reaction which can be shown to be different from those of any other emotion – as, for example, the fear that one experiences when one is anxious about having to defend oneself against false accusations of a serious crime."

I do indeed remember the particular circumstances surrounding my finding out that I my test was designated positive. Previously, my then Mother-In-Law had lapsed into a coma after a reaction to the dye inserted in her bloodstream during a routine test at Cobb Memorial Hospital in Phenix City, Alabama. My wife left her banking job in Lawton, Oklahoma and went to be with her. On every other weekend, I used to drive the fifteen hours straight from Lawton, Oklahoma to Columbus, Georgia. On return, I always drove the twelve (12) hours straight to Dallas, Texas and rested. This time, I stopped in Dallas and drank a refreshing cold 16 ounce Colt-45 Malt Liquor. I continued to take interstate highway I-35E north up to Denton, Texas where I fell onto Texas state highway 380 heading west 35 miles to Decatur, Texas. That was a truly sweet highway that literally begged your automobile to run at its best. And I had the perfect car for the journey, a Midnight Blue 1978 Lincoln Continental Mark V with 460 cu in. engine, 4-barrel carburetor, dual exhausts and oversize L78 whitewall tires.

I did not know it at the time, but the Texas Highway Patrol discreetly had me under surveillance the entire time from Denton to Decatur. After thirty-five miles, when the highway goes into Decatur, you enter the town under a railroad trestle. As I came up from under the trestle, all I could see were Blue Lights!! I was really kinda drowsy after all that driving, so I just reached under my seat to get my wallet where I had placed it when I went inside the beer joint. I really thought that it was just a routine Road Check for Driver's Licenses. **IT WAS NOT!!** When I did that, six (6) big guns came into my open windows with the six uniformed Police yelling, **"HOLD IT, HANDS UP!!!"** One trooper opened my door, snatched me out and literally threw me against the hood of my car. He demanded to know where my identification was. I told him it was under my seat. He retrieved it and began to rifle through **MY** wallet. I told him to stop and let me get what he wanted. Then another policeman again forcibly threw me against my automobile. **Now, they really got my attention!!**

I later learned that there was a mass slaying/robbery in Arlington, Texas which is between Dallas and Fort Worth. These cops focused on me to be the perpetrator since I was clocked exceeding the speed limit by several different units. Five Texas police cars had me under surveillance from Denton to Decatur. When they stopped me and discovered that I was just a soldier returning to duty, they then decided to charge me with Driving Under the Influence ,DUI, probably cas' they smelled the beer on my breath. They placed me in handcuffs, and put me into the back of a Ford Bronco. The date was January 7, 1985. I will always remember that date because the cop traveled down some extremely dark roads! And with me in shackles, I just **KNEW** I was about to be another well-beaten Black Man, so I attempted to lighten the situation by meekly exclaiming, "I thought Dr. Martin Luther King stopped this??!"

Soon after I said that the Bronco entered a clearing and we arrived at the Texas Highway Department Headquarters. When we entered, there was a menacing-looking machine about the size of a washing machine on one side of the room and the policeman gave me a straw and told me to blow. I puffed. He then sternly said that he was going to give me one more chance before he would lock me up, so, I blew until the red light on the machine lighted up. Unbeknownst to me, legally he was only supposed to run the test once. He ran the test four times. Then he started reading me Texas regulations. I then asked him was I drunk. He said I was not. (During that time the alcohol limit in Texas was .10 and I was sooooo thankful that the beer I drank earlier did not reach that level). So he got on the radio and informed the others that I was not drunk and asked what to do with me? Five cops clocked my speed. Variations went from 70 in a 55 mph zone, 60 in a 45 mph zone, 55 in a 40, and 45 in a 30. They gave me a ticket for $40.00. They took me back to my automobile which was left running. The Mexican deputy who was left with the car and his girlfriend were in <u>MY</u> car and my Lincoln had the unmistakable smell of sex. Mentally, I made up my mind to **NEVER** travel that route again!

When I got to Lawton 0500 in the morning, I had to report for work at 0745. When I attempted to angrily tell the First Sergeant what transpired, he then informed me that my urine sample that I gave November 27, 1984 came back positive.

I THEN became the first to question the results, because:

When the results were returned, my unit went to the ultimate extreme to make an example out of me because I had been a professional competent Instructor at the United States Field Artillery School at Fort Sill, Oklahoma. I knew how to instruct a classroom. My tasks included instructing Officers with the Basic Officer's Course and NCOs with the Advanced NCO course with establishing cryptographic equipment installation. I recall the intense Instructor Training Course, ITC; satisfactory completion was required before we stepped before a class. In the class with me were several officers. We had sessions where we actually had to spend twenty minutes instructing the class about the proper usage of a writing pen, or another insignificant item. Each time that we gave a presentation, we were critiqued by the remainder of the class. Most times there was very little criticism given to me, but I STILL got a final grade lower than what the officers received.

Also, I was the COMSEC Custodian for Fort Sill, the sole person responsible by hand receipt for the hundreds of cryptographic equipment on the entire Fort Sill property. I was busted from SSG/E-6 one rank to SGT/E-5. I was relegated to work in grimy, dusty basement. My pay was docked for two months. I was informed that if I provided a positive polygraph, everything would be reversed. The polygraph was scheduled on a Tuesday morning. Over the previous weekend, I went to Georgia to see my wife. I returned on Monday around 2300 hours that night. I was so hyped up, apprehensive as to whether I would be able to be 'judged' by the test, concerned that my entire career was about to be determined by an unknown test, that I did drink a pint of liquor to get some much needed rest. I arrived at Army Criminal Division, CID, at 0830 the next morning to take the test. Midway through the test, the examiner told me to go back to my unit. When I got back to my unit, I was given a breathalyzer which registered that I was above the legal limit. I was then additionally charged with being drunk on duty. I was scheduled to appear before a board of officers who were to determine my fitness for duty.

I was assigned a Trial Defense Attorney who represented me exceptionally well. What he discovered was that there were problems at the laboratory with the testing procedures. When my attorney requested that they provide proof that they sampled my urine, they could not. He sent formal requests to the laboratory and they used the fact that they were not liable to provide any proof under military law because they were contract. For this reason, the board concluded that I was to be given an Honorable Discharge, suspended for six months. The final authority to approve this decision was the Base Commander. Now, when all this **FIRST** took place, when my pay was reduced, I rushed to the military legal office, Judge Advocate General, JAG, to have them submit letters to my creditors informing them that because of matters beyond my control I would be sending them the minimum amount. And, I had superb A-1 credit. Without my knowledge, and against the decision of the board to suspend actions for six months, the Base Commander made the abrupt decision to have me 'kicked out' of the army within ten days, so the same legal folk sent additional correspondence to the **SAME** creditors informing them that they no longer represented me because I was separated from the army.

When I arrived at my residence, an eleven- room house on a corner in downtown Lawton, my front porch was filled with representatives from **ALL** my creditors demanding to be paid, **NOW!** When I saw this, an epiphany came to me! **Bankruptcy**! When I filed this, nothing short of a miracle could describe the feeling of elation this brought. The army continued extending their derision of me by actually escorting me to the front gate with the instructions to never again step foot on a military base. **I REALLY, TRULY FELT ASHAMED, DISGRACED! WORDS CAN NEVER DESCRIBE MY FEELINGS OF DISPAIR.** The only album that allowed me to survive was Earth, Wind &Fire, **"That's the Way of the World"**. I listened to that cassette, religiously:

> *"A child is born with a heart of Gold, but the <u>Way of the World</u> makes his heart so Cold!"*

The Army paid for my civilian attorney. He filed a lawsuit(contending that the discharge was unlawful. I later discovered he was really paid to get me back onto active duty. When I got to my home in Charleston, South Carolina, two days later I received a letter from the Pentagon stating that the Department Of Army was inviting me back onto active duty I actually had to drive my automobile back to the bankruptcy court in Lawton, turn over ownership of my beloved Mark V, and return to Charleston on a Greyhound bus. That was a terribly shameful feeling. My parent's, even though they never acknowledged it, saw me as a failure because my Father was in the Navy during World War II and had retired after twenty-six years with the United States Postal Service. My older brother who was an aircraft technician in the navy had only recently retired from civil service repairing C-17s, large cargo planes, at Charleston Air Force base, and my older sister was a Ph. D. candidate, educator.

My Father died one week later, so I forgot about army. Depression got the better of me; I avoided family and so-called friends. One night a faithful first-cousin of mine, Richard, took me to a night club where I met this Lady who fascinated me with her loveliness. We danced the remainder of the night until the club closed about two A.M., then went to my cousin's apartment in the projects and made **MAD** Love until daylight. She introduced me to the captivating joys of marijuana. I figured since I was already labeled a 'druggie', ... what the hell!! I took her home, which happened to be on the same street where I was born, and we made **MAD** Love again, and again for the rest of the day! WE had a relationship where we made Love for eighty-nine days, straight! This Lady was previously a Ms. Black Charleston with five kids, and she had an unbelievable insatiable sexual appetite. Each time we made Love she had to reach orgasm, three times. I ate a bounty of oysters, consumed plenty of raw eggs, drank a lot of gin, and smoked heaps & heaps of marijuana; everything possible to enable me to satisfy her unquenchable, voracious craving. This bliss pacified me for a while yet there still was this nagging, lingering feeling of failure that continued to haunt me. The funny way our overture ended is tied to the way our lovemaking sessions commenced. Always on her third 'stairway to heaven', this vociferous Lady had the tendency to be loud enough for her neighbor to hear. After a while, when she would leave me fully exhausted in bed while she left the residence, probably to further assuage her healthy appetite elsewhere, the "curious" female neighbor started to always knock on the door to 'use' the telephone. Heaven knows I would be left naked, and physically unable, but, Faith acted like I guess any women would under the circumstances; suspicious. To put an end to the wariness, I placed **BOTH** women together and spoke to them regarding the precarious situation. I do not think it worked!! Faith has since remarried, but, we will forever remain friends.

VI. Re-Entry- Back into the FIRE

Finally, after eight months, I contacted an attorney in Charleston who informed me that because they gave me an Honorable Discharge while charged with **Gross Misconduct, Illegal Drug Possession and Drunk on Duty,** they literally cleared the way for me to reenlist. The Honorable Discharge was technically an invitation. Since this was done, any litigation would be futile. I told my 'paid attorney' that I would reenter, but only if I could be stationed at Fort Benning, Georgia, near where my wife's Mother remained comatose.

The Pentagon suggested Redstone Arsenal, Huntsville, Alabama, but that was not an option. It was soon agreed that I would be assigned to Fort Benning, which is adjacent to Phenix City Alabama. I did not know it, but I was literally **SNEAKED** back into the army. Earlier, a Major at the Pentagon called me and told me to **NOT** discuss the settlement with anyone or it would be voided. They sent the Final Settlement by Registered Mail. I signed and returned the settlement. I came to Columbus and reunited with my wife.

To reenter the army, I was taken to Opelika, Alabama, then to Montgomery, Alabama. When I finally arrived at Fort Benning, the position I was given was Assistant to the Inspector General for the largest Infantry Brigade in the United States Army, 3000 soldiers, at Kelley Hill, 197th Infantry Brigade. I never received any training for the job position I held in the Inspector General's Office. Yet, I performed in this capacity superbly. I was responsible for the management of personnel concerns. These issues included military, personal or financial problems. My clientele included active-duty and their family members.

I readily recall the first Inspector General Action Request I worked. A Sp4/E-4 who entered the army earlier under a newer version of the GI bill met a young lady and he wanted to get married. However, the GI bill he signed when he entered deducted a specified amount from his paycheck monthly and then when he would separate from the service, the army would pay two dollars for every dollar he saved. Still, the soldier was in Love. I interviewed him, went to personnel to review his file and ensure that he did not have any administrative actions pending in his files, which he did not. I then worked to get the soldier a satisfactory answer to his request. Regulations dictated that a reply, if not final, was to be supplied to the client within thirty days. Within that thirty-day period, I acted on that case ceaselessly. I even spoke to the Colonel at the military personnel center in Alexandria, Virginia, MILPERCEN, who authored the bill. When I spoke about the circumstances surrounding the soldier's request and fact that it seemed to be a divisive issue to take pay when the potential exists that situations just might change, the Colonel/author agreed with me, and the bill was amended, the soldier got his money, got married, and reenlisted. This was only the first of over 500 IGARs I acted on during my assignment with the Inspector General office.

I began experiencing some strange pay problems when I went active, again. I would get a check for $8,000.00, and some wise finance clerk would make the 'wise' decision that I was overpaid. This happened several times and this truly made my existence complicated since I was directed to not discuss the reactivation with anyone. Once, I was actually dropped from the rolls for sixty days, but, I still managed to not let my personal problems interfere with my IG responsibilities. I took extreme pride in my position as Assistant to the Inspector General.

The Inspector General is the liaison between commanders and soldiers, and part of his mission is to interpret army rules and regulations for concerned soldiers and or dependents. Another familiar case was when a unit was scheduled to attend National Training Center in the desert in California. The young soldier claimed to be claustrophobic. The captain asked the IG office whether it was legal to drug the soldier, place him on the plane, and then take him to California. I deeply researched this. According to pertinent regulations, it was illegal to drug the soldier to make him do something he would otherwise refuse to do. The soldier did not go to NTC. I assume that administrative actions, separation papers were initiated.

One memorable incident occurred on Kelley Hill that I think about to this day. Every morning, Kelley Hill closes at 0500 for Physical Training, PT. One morning during mandatory training a soldier had an asthma attack and his unit took him to the unit's medical facilities where there happened to be a Physician Assistant, PA, on duty. Instead of evacuating this soldier to the nearby hospital, two miles away, he treated the soldier. If the soldier was transported, this would have required an ambulance which would have had the potential to totally interrupt Kelley Hill's morning Physical Training. The soldier died. This death triggered an Inspector General Investigation. The investigation discovered that the PA did not properly attend to the dying soldier's needs. I became truly upset. Yet I was constrained by regulations against divulging the results of an IG investigation. It really takes an act of Congress to get that information. On another unrelated matter I spoke directly with the soldier's Mother, and, as hard as it was, I was not able to tell her that she could get millions for the wrongful death of her child; and then witness her receive a paltry $50,000.00 in survivor's benefits.

Another humorous incident occurred one morning as I entered Kelley Hill, home of the 197th Infantry Brigade. Someone hit a skunk and his fumes had the entire back side of Kelley Hill 'humming'. As it was, different battalions were responsible monthly for daily Police Call, cleanup. I checked the roster, and called the Sergeant Major, SGM, of the battalion. This soldier probably was probably in the army twice as long as I, so it was partially understood the animosity he displayed during the call. Since me, an E-6 was telling him, an E-9, to do what his battalion was scheduled to do, he somewhat resented this, so he asked me again what was my rank? I simply reminded that I was calling from the Inspector General's Office. That ended the conversation, and the skunk was removed, promptly. I enjoyed this job… The Inspector General Course opened at Fort Belvoir, Virginia the winter of 1986. Because of the way I performed, I was selected to attend the course for three weeks. I decided to drive since I had driven between Washington and Charleston, South Carolina many times while stationed at Vint Hill Farms Station, Virginia. But, this time, it snowed on me from Charlotte, North Carolina all the way to Washington, DC.

Driving at night in the snow is frightening!!! It's like a swarm of baseballs continuously coming at your windshield! Since I did not have snow tires on my Lincoln, I merely let some of the air out of the tires and that allowed me to slowly make it all the way to the front gate to Fort Belvoir located in Alexandria, Virginia. The front gate on U.S. Highway 1 has a slight incline. The **ONLY** problem I encountered since Charlotte was attempting to drive up the snowy hill at 0400 in the morning before the snow plows started to roll! I then went to a nearby 'Waffle House' restaurant where I rested until daylight. Around 0730, I called the contact number given to us if we had problems. Unbeknownst to me, the number terminated within the Pentagon Inspector General Office, and to my amazement, the Army Inspector General answered the phone. Thinking I was late for the class, I started to make apologies when he abruptly stopped me and informed me that I was the **ONLY** student assigned to the class that actually made it the first day. This really made me feel great!! My rank at that time was Staff Sergeant/E6. Not only was I the lowest ranking student assigned, I was the only Black assigned. Every other student was either a MSG/E-8 and above or Captains/O-3 and Majors/O-4.

The Inspector General of the Army was a Black Man. LTG Thomas was his name. He was so impressed with my determination to get to the school that he made the decision to have me attend the eight-week course instead of the three-week one originally scheduled. Completion of the eight-week course would allow me to be locked-in to my Fort Benning assignment until I retired. This meant that a background investigation had to be completed. Students for the Inspector General Course were lodged in Penthouses. We each were assigned our very own ultra-luxury apartment in a high-rise building in Alexandria, Virginia. I really admired the way I would enter the apartment, and a mere touch of a button would cause the fireplace to function and cascade the dwelling with warmth. **I felt on top of the world!!** Nobody on earth could shatter the way I felt when I awakened each morning. They gave us an allotment from finance wherein we could shop at the humongous Safeway downstairs. I felt great as I proudly walked the aisles preparing to stock my dwelling with great food.

The third day… The third day was a beautiful sunny day. But, it was extremely cold, so cold that the snow along the sidewalks was beginning to look like huge, ugly mini glaciers, the way that it was stacked by the city's snow machines. When I awoke, I grabbed a bacon sandwich and an ice-cold coke, my own way to get a caffeine rush, on my way to class at the Pentagon. As soon as I entered the classroom, before I was able to even get my seat warm, the Instructor directed me to the Commandant's Office. I would be lying if I did not say that with the way my Life was 'Flying High', I kinda always had apprehensions about the entire legal case because it just seemed too good to be true!! As soon as I entered the Colonel/Commandant's Suite, he vocally pounced on me like I had viciously raped his

White daughter!! **<u>GET OUTA HERE!!! NOW!!!</u>** As I said, it was just too god to be true… Being an experienced employee of the IG office, I immediately requested that I be allowed to complete an IGAR, Inspector General Action Request. <u>This was my right!</u> Plus, that would have allowed me to remain in the school while the investigation took place. This Colonel looked me directly in my eyes and told me to complete my IGAR when I got back to Fort Benning. I begun to shatter.

There was a Liquor Store besides the Safeway adjacent to my high-rise. I bought a fifth of 'Smirnoff' Vodka and went into my house to drown my sorrows. The next morning, I awoke and drove directly to MILPERCEN, Military Personnel Center, which was also located in Alexandria, Virginia without a GPS, only word of mouth directions. I then went inside up to the fifth floor and queried why it was that I had to be dismissed from such a coveted school? The E-5/SGT soldier told me what I knew deep down in my gut, "The required background investigation uncovered derogatory information which prohibited attendance at the IG School." At this moment in my Life it became crystal-clear that there was a conspiracy in place towards me. I had in my possession a signed Federal Court Settlement, dated November 22, 1985 which stated that **ALL** information pertaining to the incident at Fort Sill, Oklahoma was to be deleted from my records, and, there was to be no listed break in service. **<u>Evidently, this was not done.</u>**

I had been the recipient of a Top Secret Special Intelligence security clearance and any discrepancies would have caused my clearance status to be blemished. I never had any problems, so, to have this thrust upon me most certainly allowed me to narrow down the source. I drove the 500 miles back to Columbus, Georgia as a hurt broken man… As I was driving back, reflecting on what had transpired since returning to active duty; it became obvious the pay problems I was subjected to were directly associated with the disregard that DA displayed in regards to the Settlement. To add insult to my injury, I had earlier received a response to a Army Board for Records correction which stipulated that my denial for request to be reinstated was upheld. To take so long to understand, I must have been 'Boo-Boo the Klown' to go through all that and not recognize that something was amiss.

Yet, I Thanked God that he fixed it so that I was positioned in the Inspector General Office upon reentry wherein I had access to **ALL** army regulations. The IG position permitted me to unveil the plot wherein I would most likely be discharged before retirement attributed to the derogatory information overtly left in my files. When I called my 'Paid Attorney' to inform him what happened and request that the settlement be declared null and void, he acted like he represented DA!! He refused to do as I asked. That was when I truly felt targeted, marked, defamed. I was not allowed to work again in an Inspector General Office.

The snowball of inconsistencies I experienced since returning to active duty began to increase at a rapidly uncontrollable pace. I filed an IGAR regarding the incident at the Pentagon; I received the response dated October 17, 1987. There was an investigation done regarding the incident and it was concluded that a review of my official files confirmed that army had not fully complied with Federal Court Settlement. They further concluded that the claim that the Colonel refused to accept my Inspector General Action Request was unsubstantiated. Now, I had two years experience working in the IG office. I CLEARED over 600 IGARs. I **knew how an IGAR worked and its expediency. Was it not logical that faced with unsolicited complications, I would probably be FIRST to submit an IGAR!!??** This further cemented my realization that I was doomed.

While I displayed keen insight disposing of problems brought to me via IGARs, I was totally ignorant with what was happening to me. Money concerns were mounting rapidly. Because I could not work in the IG office again, and, attributed to the fact that my clearance was lifted, I was assigned to work in the Judge Advocate General Office. My task was to assist with the preparation of legal defense cases for service members. I did not realize it at the time, but, this position allowed me to become familiar with the required format for lawsuits, an ability that would be required later. I worked in this capacity for eight months. I found out just how valuable this experience was when I was given a ticket by the Military Police on day as I left Fort Benning. A squad car was positioned near the front gate as I approached a stop sign. I was given the ticket because the cop acknowledged that I stopped behind a car at the stop sign. He gave me the ticket because he claims that I ran the stop sign since I did not move forward and stop again. This was ludicrous!! Instead of paying the $50.00 Federal ticket as I was advised to do by the JAG office attorneys, I decided to fight the case myself. During this time, $50.00 might as well had been $50,000.00, with all the money problems I was having…The first thing I did was to use one of those cheap Polaroid cameras that self-developed pictures to take a picture from the four different corners, including the one where the MP was located. I then purchased a large white poster board and drew the intersection with indications where my Lincoln was in regards to the small automobile in front of me. When I got to the courthouse, I felt confident that at the least I would be able to give the judge a reasonable doubt. During my hearing, when I informed the judge that the corner in question involved the Military Police daily reversing two lanes of travel to accommodate incoming/outgoing auto traffic, and, they used removable devices to control. I contended that while I did stop behind the compact car, a Ford Pinto that was ahead of me, I still had complete view of the intersection because the Pinto was not stopped properly. The removable sign bisected the driver's door. When I told this to the judge, he dismissed the case.

Two weeks later I was reclassified into the medical field. The job I was given was Patient Administration. I take pride to do my utmost in whatever capacity I am assigned. Working in an army hospital enabled me to help soldiers who truly, no doubt about it, needed help! And yes, the mounting money problems continued to haunt my Life… I felt like an Albatross had attached itself to me.

Still unable to control my pay problems, my new NCOIC , a SFC Reedy, who had only just met me, took it upon himself to erroneously conclude that the reason behind my money problems was that I was taking care of another family. My unit then started administrative paperwork to get me discharged for 'Financial Instability'. He even had the audacity to call my then wife on her job at a local bank and tell her this. I feel his tactic for this was to throw a curve in the mix with the intention to distract me while the paperwork travelled through the system. Since we were not on the best of terms, my wife failed to tell me in a timely fashion what Reedy had done. When she did tell me two weeks before my second discharge, all efforts to deal with Reedy seemed pointless, but I did take her to the Military Police Station to prepare a sworn statement denoting the action. Then, I just gave it to God, and let Him handle it.

I was again discharged with a 'General Discharge under Honorable Conditions' on 20Jun90. I know 'Boo-Boo' the klown can see the association between the first discharge which included bankruptcy and forfeitures, and the second which was preceded by severe pay problems to include being dropped from the rolls for sixty (60) days. I did not realize it but I was beginning to have mental setbacks related to the Organic Brain Syndrome diagnosis provided me in 1977 at Walter Reed Hospital. Attributed to vast money problems, and the lie perpetrated by my NCOIC, we lost the house we moved in when I reentered the army in 1985, and my wife left me again.

I was absolutely miserable. I felt lonely, lost, friendless, abandoned, isolated… After being the holder of the highest security clearance attainable, then to be wrongfully discharged twice from the army, followed by watching myself being brought to utter disgrace, I just could not go bring myself to go back to Charleston. I walked the streets of Columbus like a zombie. I did not know how to find a shelter. I became reclusive. I slept a couple of nights under the railroad trestle beside St. James AME Church on 11th Street. I used to sleep in parked Greyhound Buses parked by the nearby bus station at night. I slept regularly in a truck with a sleeper cab parked on Martin Luther King, Jr. Boulevard at Weathers Brothers Moving and Storage.

I was beginning to feel reluctantly comfortable with my existence. I had earlier learned about the Soup Kitchen located at the Catholic Church Fellowship Hall on Veterans Parkway and 12th Street. The hardest thing I have ever had to do in my Life was stand in a Soup Line on a busy street awaiting free food. **I felt so ashamed!** I felt like everybody I knew in this world was traveling down Veterans Parkway. Yet, after just two days, 2 really hungry days, I became a professional Soup Line Member! Mentally, I was seriously gullible… On the way to the Soup Kitchen one morning, I passed a building at the corner of Fifth Avenue and 12th Street. There was a poster in a window boasting that Commercial Drivers would make in excess of $40,000.00 the first year. hmmmmmm. *I immediately thought this to be a Godsend!*

After breakfast one morning, I returned to the same building on the corner of 12th Street and 5th Avenue and commenced to complete paperwork to start making $40,000.00 and once again return to the level of Life I once knew. When the representative discovered that I was a veteran, this seemed to make his sales pitch that more in-depth. The school was to be in Montgomery, Alabama, and was scheduled to start in 45 days. My problem… How do I get there???!

I remember when I was in the army working Patient Administration at Martin Army Community Hospital, Fort Benning, I met a truly lovely, fantastic Lady. One of my daily tasks at the hospital involved patient accountability. This entailed walking throughout this large hospital and counting patients within each ward on all floors. Several times as I would walk down the hallways, impeccably dressed in my Class A's, I would come across one beautiful nurse, Ms. Bobbie Carolyn Harper. She walked with an aura of sophistication about her, and I was straight away attracted to this.

We seemed to bond almost immediately! As time went on, when I would have troublesome situations, as I most times always did, she was **ALWAYS** an open ear to my innermost, deepest discussions. Out of shame, I neglected to talk with her since being discharged from the army a second time. I figured that any minute this nightmare would end; all the time not fully realizing the magnitude of the loss I had suffered. Yet, with the idea that I was presented with the opportunity to get back on my feet quick, I approached Bobbie with my proposal.

Lo and behold, as soon as I presented her with my intentions to attend truck-driving school in Montgomery, she lovingly agreed to let me borrow one of her automobiles to drive to the school. First, I had to apply for an upgrade of my discharge wherein I would be able to utilize my earned educational benefits. This happened rather quickly because I simply filled out DD form 293 and after three months I received the upgraded discharge. Life was beginning to shine once again!!! I went to the Driver's Licensing facility in Columbus to obtain my Commercial Drivers License, CDL permit. This required the successful completion of five written tests. I spent two weeks studying the informative CDL manual. I returned, passed all five tests and obtained my CDL permit.

I drove to Montgomery. Alabama and started to immerse myself into the classroom instructions because I Loved trucks since my postal worker Father brought me my first toy metal tractor-trailer truck, "Fill-Up with Billups". So, I really felt that whatever transpired in my past, all those sour events, was just preparation for the $40,000.00 I was about to make. I was soooooo wrong. After five days of classroom instructions, we would daily pack the truck with six students and an instructor and go on the road. Each day, we would stop at the same Truck Stop to eat breakfast. This would encompass two hours. This was also troublesome to me since I had no money. Then we would go around the block twice and return for a two hour lunch. This went on the entire time that I was there.

Finally, one day when we anticipated the start of classes, we had none. Apparently, the school closed without notifying the students. So, this actually triggered a response within me wherein I ended up in an inner-city project in Montgomery where I commenced to self-medicate myself with readily available devil/crack. What I eventually learned was that the school, 'Diesel Academy' was a scam set up to elicit school loan money from susceptible students. And, what made this scam so sweet is that the student is the ONLY person recognized when damages are assessed. And, Student Loan debt stays with you until you die! Bankruptcy will not even dismiss Federal School Loan debt. And the interest quickly, rapidly, mounts!!

I recall when I was a young man in Charleston, SC, that there was this office of the government whose sole purpose was to review schools before they got approval to accept money from students. Evidently this office was the victim of a 'shotgun' budget cutbacks, 'cas I have gone to every authoritative person I could find, United States Representatives, Congressmen, lawyers, judges, paralegals, etc. Each time I get sooo much sympathy, but still would leave feeling like 'Boo-Boo the fool' for falling into a trap so blatantly foul. I was made to feel that it was **MY** responsibility to check the school before I allowed them to get $15,000.00 in my name from the government. Yes, ultimately I do accept some blame for this fiasco, but, to be presented with a program that outwardly looks legitimate should have been checked out thoroughly by **MY** government simply since only the government has the resources to accomplish such a task. Think about it! If those scam schools, and there have been many, were required to be examined by the government, then when students violate, the blame surely should be assigned.

But, to have any sly quick scammer devise a plan that hoodwinks the government and takes money under which vulnerable, gullible students are indebted forever is unreal and sets a sorry precedent. Additionally, this caused significant disillusionment with the dreams I so dearly carried while also multiplying the disgrace I felt. …**BUT**, here comes that devil/crack…

Faced with this newest dilemma, I literally went berserk! I started to steal. And, I was never a good thief. Actually, I believe I stole as an attempt to cry out for help!! I was thirty-eight the first time I went to jail. And, five minutes in jail is tooooo long!!! I first went to jail in Montgomery, Alabama charged with theft by taking. In Alabama if you do not own property you cannot make bail unless you pay cash. Bobbie informed my brother in Charleston about my plight and he came to Montgomery to bail me out. Once I got out, I was so out of it, so sick, I actually stole again three days later. Well, this time, I had to spend four months in jail. Those were extremely hectic four months. I was thirty-eight, and in a jail-cell with 65 other Black Men from the Montgomery metropolitan area with various gang affiliations. The bulk of them were charged with drug offenses. Apparently, members of a rival gang from Jamaica were intruding into the local gangs turf and this produced violence. Everyone I would talk to, if they did not know me previously would assume that I am from Jamaica, or another West Indian island because of my accent/dialect. Soooo, while being confined for four months, I fought nearly every day because these young gang-bangers just knew I was one of those reviled Jamaica Boys. Fighting in jail ain't too bad 'cas the only weapons readily available in the County lockup are the orange rubber slippers given to prisoners upon arrival or the rubber food trays. None of these were lethal. I fought so much until I was placed in solitary confinement for twenty-one days. And, that was an extremely **COLD** twenty-one day incarceration, with no blanket!

The day I went to court was the day that I was released, and the day I left Alabama. I came back to Columbus, confused, distraught and unfeeling. Now, I was further unable to return to my hometown with this new stigma I carry. To compound the disdain I felt, the investigative television show, "60 Minutes" broadcast a segment on **<u>Shoplifting</u>** which actually was a stage for these white folk to glossily faddishly explain why they felt the need to steal. I felt insulted!! Here I was, a classified recidivist, a felon, marked for Life, and these white folks are on television acting like it's a trend of some sort. For the second time, I wrote to "Dateline". And, further proof that **GOD** is **GOD**: during my devil/crack days, when I had access to a car, I would always provide transportation to a dealer in exchange for a piece of devil/crack.

When I think about it, I risked my entire LIFE providing transportation because if we were stopped, even though the dealer ALWAYS would tell you that he would claim the contraband, odds are that I would be charged; and with the quantities that he carried, I could have been charged with 'Intent to Distribute'!! Anyway, that devil/crack had a way of making you feel invincible, so all times of the night I would ferry drug dealers and drug users to get devil/crack. One fellow, younger than my child, who I allowed to befriend me, would provide me with devil/crack to take him around town. Once he asked for a suggestion for a gift for his girlfriend for Valentine's Day. Being the 'Know-it All' I was known to be, I suggested that he buy her a negligee and some perfume. So, we went to a shop where local strippers purchased their attire. I figured that he most certainly would be able to find something appealing. While I walked around the store commenting on different items, he feigned shyness and after fifteen minutes, he decided against buying a nightie.

I forgot this incident. After three years, when I had already been to jail several times, classified a recidivist wherein if I steal a box of matches I can be sent to jail for ten years, Columbus Police Department decided to clear up old arrest warrants. I had just gotten a room at a 'better' high-rise living facility for the disabled, and, lo and behold there was an arrest warrant for me. On Wednesday, August 11, 2010 at 1200 PM, as I was watching television, I was interrupted by two Columbus city detectives who informed me that they held two (2) warrants for my arrest. Of course I was stunned, but, I KNEW that resistance would only be futile, and cause unnecessary embarrassment, so, I asked them what I was about to be arrested for??!! They said that the warrants stated that I went into 'Night Moves' in the 4800 block of Armour Road and walked out one day with four(4) 'Bustiers'. I then went in another day and took another. I started to protest and as the detectives took one step into my room he got a whiff of the joint I had just smoked in the bathroom. Soooo he stated that either I was going to go quietly or he was gonna call for the dogs!! OKAY!!

I felt that once we were at the Police Station, the matter would be resolved in my favor; however, when we got there the detectives went in, and, the detectives came back to the car where I had my huge body squeezed, while handcuffed, into a 26 x 48 inch area, he then discovered that the warrants were dated 2007!! I truly felt that this was reason for me to be released, but, I was told that I had to see a judge to be released. I was taken to the city jail, where I was forced to sleep on the floor. I KNEW that I would be able to resolve this when I spoke to the judge on Thursday morning. Thursday morning came & went, and, I was forced to sleep on the floor of the cellblock for another night. When Friday morning came, I was then informed that I would not be able to see the judge until 2:00 PM. NOTE: I DID NOT SLEEP AT ALL SINCE BEING ARRESTED. EACH & EVERY MINUTE WAS SPENT SEARCHING MY MIND FOR ANYTHING, ANYTHING THAT I DID IN 2007 TO HAVE ME ARRESTED IN SUCH A LAME MANNER. I FOUND NOTHING. When Friday came and I was allowed to appear before a judge, as soon as I entered the courtroom, the judge was informed that the city declined to prosecute for lack of evidence. I later learned that the City Policeman who wrote the warrant was in the Reserves and directly after he wrote the warrant he was deployed to Afghanistan where he was killed. That is the only reason why I am not sitting a jail cell right now feeling like 'Boo-Boo the Fool', 'cas I believe that when I tried to befriend a criminal and took him to get something for his sweetie, while he pretended shyness he actually was concealing the negligees on his person, and the white females in the store simply looked out the window and copied my tag number! Evidently, there was not enuff evidence or the warrant would not have sat as long as it did even though the policeman was deployed, now dead. Yet, attributed to the fact that I had more than three convictions for Theft by Taking, Shoplifting, I risked ten (10) years in jail.

I believe that this whole incident was contrived by the devil and that is why it had ended as it did. GOD has better plans for me!! This is another reason why I choose the church. Earlier I was truly offended when the investigative program, "Dateline" broadcast a segment on 'Shoplifting'. They practically glamorized this action by the white 'victims'. I had to respond:

13 November 1998
#2 South Theri Court
Henry Alston Gaillard
Columbus, GA

Dateline
PERSONAL FOR; Mr. Neal Shipiro
30 Rockefeller Plaza
New York, New York
REFERENCE: NBC Correspondence dated 01 November 1998

NOTE: No Reply Necessary

Dear Mr. Shipiro:

I sincerely regret that it is impossible for "Dateline" to investigate this exigent state. However, after watching tonight's show, I feel the need to vent. My only request is that you read this letter.

Tonight, Dateline broadcast a segment produced by Andi Gitow about shoplifting; the compulsion, the lasting effects, and possible treatment. While I do not intend to attempt to ask you to modify your decision, I **MUST** respond:

To further expound on my situation, when I eventually became homeless after I lost everything dear to me because of baseless slanderous charges, I lapsed into a downward spiral of depression. I stole food to eat. I stole sleeping pills to be able to get some rest since sleep escaped me. Now, stealing is wrong. Yet maybe because I was unable, after an extended period of time, to get any sort of assistance, my thefts could very well have been, "cries for help". **The 'Therapy' I get each and every time I enter a store is the knowledge that the next time I steal even a Bubble Gum I will get seven, (7) years behind bars. Ain't nuttin' glamorous 'bout dat!** Everything I stole was less than $25.00, which means that all three should have been misdemeanors. However, with the way the law is written in Georgia, I am now a convicted felon. I Love trucks. As I was in the midst of my personal turmoils, and somewhat vulnerable, I got involved with a bogus Truck Driving School. If I had been more mentally alert at the time, I would've been able to foresee that the school was no more than a scam set up to fraudulently obtain Federal Student Loan monies from the government via gullible students. At This time, I still receive letters from the U.S. Department of Education demanding that I send them over $5,000.00. I never received my license. The school has since closed. I studied, on my own to obtain my Commercial Driver's License, CDL, permit. I consider myself to be a competent driver, but, I still require a road test. I cannot gain employment in this field with any of the major carriers since they travel to Canada and, you may not cross the border with a felony. I am eligible for re-hire with the Federal Government. Yet, I cannot utilize the 15 years 4 months I invested toward retirement because felony convictions prohibit employment. MY ten year window closes on 05 July 1999. Three weeks ago I was discharged from a minimum wage job washing trucks because of my felony convictions. **Now when I go to job interviews, I might just as well have robbed a bank!!**

Now, maybe I did not use the right words in my correspondence, or maybe I did not know the right people to get NBC's attention to my plight. I do know that from a fiscal standpoint, s segment designated to me would have encompassed several pertinent, recent issues. Some possible topics you could have used:

A. **Everybody Plays the Fool**- How a Man who held the highest security clearance attainable is kicked-out of the army twice, wrongfully. (DA insured that a Non-Disclosure Agreement, NDA, for 75 years was signed)
B. **Golden Showers**- What will occur when a urinalysis test is administered wrong and the long-term devastating effects, especially if you are Black.
C. **Violence is the Tool of the Ignorant**- What causes some people to become homicidal over personal employment issues and why it is that I just utilize persistent, persuasive perseverance. (This one would've saved many lives!!)
D. **God Bless America**- Why it is that the majority of traitors who "sold out' this country are white and why this Black Man who is the holder of some of the most sensitive secrets this country has was degraded, debased, and defamed, remains steadfast in his respect for his debriefing statement. **I never ever even thought about selling secrets!! (Love of Country)**

E. **It's a Shame-** How being a convicted felon rearranges your Life.
F. **A Child is Born with a Heart Of Gold, but, the Way of The World Makes His Heart So Cold-** America has these supposedly "edumacated" individuals who are addressing the drug epidemic in the **WRONG** way. When I was homeless, sleeping in abandoned cars, under buildings; when I reluctantly arrived at the conclusion that all was over, I had my first encounter with illegal substances. Drugs are a frame of mind. When there is no hope, there is **ALWAYS** dope!! This may have very well have been a suppression tactic directed at keeping down the masses and it indeed did get out of hand. Once a person realizes that his/her Life has direction, when a person can live that Life within the limits of the law without fear of wrongful persecution; when justice, competent justice can be afforded by all, we will have a significantly less drug problem.

All of the above suggested topics have been done not from a hypothetical stage, but from first-hand knowledge. All I wanted was my name back.

For your information, I have been diligent in my quest for justice in this matter. Prior to contact with NBC, I contacted a supposed prominent attorney who understood Military Law. I showed him the exact same packet that I sent to you. **Again**, I received a negative response.

SINCERELY
Henry A. Gaillard

V. Homeless

I went to housing and applied for a room at the local Single-Room-Occupancy, SRO, flophouse, The Joe House. When I moved the room there, men and women, both, were occupants. There was sixty rooms, and fifteen bathrooms. **NINETY-NINE PERCENT OF THE RESIDENTS SMOKED DEVIL/CRACK.** The **ONLY** person I soon learned did not smoke was Buster. Buster LOVED food tooooo much to develop a crack/devil habit. And, **Buster COULD EAT!!!!** Buster loved Black women, Buster used to work cleanup at the nearby McDonald's, and, there he became acquainted with a female who lived in the projects of Phenix City. That did not last too long 'cas the female told us she left Buster to watch her 18 month old son while she went to the store, and, when she came back she **SAW** Buster eating the baby's Peas & Ham, out of the jar!! Buster could eat!!

    Another fella I figured did not indulge was the local 'snitch'. We called him 'Greasyhead'! We called him Greasyhead because he would daily put an overabundance of hair grease in his head in an attempt to acquire his own-style process. He had a habit of lurking around folk's doors, then he would meet a certain police officer blocks away from Joe House and tattle. Everyone there did dirt. Greasy-head used to court disabled females, and he was partial to the ones who got a disability check. He also had a habit of going to different storefront churches and ply his 'homeless woes", telling them he needs help to pay his rent. (His rent like the rest of us was paid by the city) Most times those Christian GOD-fearing folk would take up a collection to place in his hands. What he did with that money is something I cannot tell you because he got **ALL** his clothes from the 'House of Mercy', and his food from the meals at The local Salvation Army!!

    Then there was Bernard. This was one extremely stupid individual who somehow happened to have acquired a college degree. Just how he did that remains a mystery. I moved in before him. One night he came downstairs, called 911 on the old-style coin telephone, then went back upstairs and laid down on the floor in the center of his room. Apparently he was trying to document incidents so as to help him get his disability check. When the tiny female EMT arrived and passed the phone downstairs on her way to his room, her first question was, "If you're on the floor, just how were you able to get downstairs to dial 911??!!"

    Right across from my room was this couple that lived in side-by-side rooms. She was White and he was Black. Now, this bald-headed Black dude had a SERIOUS crack/devil habit!! The way he figured, if he would allow his lady friend to 'entertain' (prostitute) herself to sustain his cocaine habit, he'd always have an ample amount to smoke. He actually thought that he was Kool when he did it!!! That is just the extent of where that drug relegates you…

His ruse went on for awhile, but, one day while she was 'dealing' with this elderly white guy the owner of the building decided to have an unannounced inspection. The owner figured out what was going on and used the label of 'Health & Welfare" to enter the room where he discovered the lady on her knees!

And who can ever forget Dino!! Dino was an avid mouthwash drinker. He was about seventy+ years old and his family would send him pocket money to buy cigarettes, etc. Anyway, the manager of Joe House had a habit of seizing Dino's mail, and using the money for his own habit. When Dino learned of this is the day I met Dino. I was laying in my room after taking a hit of Devil/Crack when I heard someone loudly screaming, **"I'M GONNA KICK YOUR BIG BLACK ASS!!** When I opened the door, al I saw was this tiny white man with a comical appearance, who probably weighed 87 pounds fully wet. I actually had to hold him back from jumping on the 'manager'. Back then an assault on the manager was automatic eviction. Anyway, as I calmed Dino down, I learned that he was one very likeable guy whose Life took unavoidable turns which resulted in his living in Joe House. He soon became one of my best friends…

Incidents such as these are daily goings on in the Joe House. Like any segment of society, there is a hierarchy to homelessness. Like any class of people, there are some that can and some that cannot.

Crack/Devil devastates anything it comes in contact with. I do believe within my soul that this destructive, controlling substance was developed by a madman to be used to manipulate/dominate a specific segment of this society because it works entirely too well!! It's not like what it does to one person will not happen to the next, Devil/Crack works the same on everybody, no matter what you may have been taught, no matter what color or ethnic origin you possess.

The real separation factor is the more money you have, the more Devil/Crack you gonna smoke and probably overdose. ….I constantly fought with my inner self about being under controlled /enslaved by that vile every day I promised myself that I would someday conquer this demon!! But it just felt so **DAMN GOOD!!!** That's the hook for this Devil/Master! Making you feel soooooo good while it completely rips apart your entire existence!! And, **ALL** the women in Joe House indulged, so a person with funds could party until his money runs out. Then the female would go to the next person with money or dope.

This cycle went on 24/7. Life there was a never-ending party!! All I had to do was wait for my unemployment check to be delivered. And in between checks, I would sell blood or Food Stamps; anything to get money to be with these ladies, two or three at a time. The few times when I had no money and no crack/devil, I would Pray to **GOD** to rid me of this devil. I started to Pray because I knew that outside of being placed on another planet in a far off solar system, only **GOD** could get me away from this vile/evil substance.

I then got a scare that really opened my eyes to the demise I was bringing onto myself. Early one morning, When I went to the Blood Bank that was on Dillingham Street in Phenix City, I attempted to sell some more Plasma so as to get some more Crack/Devil. Yet, this time after the preliminary checkup, the nurse told me that I would have to wait until the Doctor came in before I could participate. This had **NEVER** happened to me ever since I was selling Blood, so a million different thoughts ran rampantly through my mind with the **FIRST** and foremost being that I had contracted HIV. **(Da package)** The Blood Bank was directly next to a bridge and I walked back and forth across that bridge maybe 46 times, each step contemplating jumping into the water after the Doctor gave me the dreaded diagnosis. When the Doctor came in and called me, he took his professional time as he started to read the nurse's report to me. He then said I had contracted Syphilis! **SYPHILIS??!! (WHEW!!) I STARTED TO SHAKE HIS HAND!!** I truly felt relief 'cause I know they discovered a cure for syph'!! I still questioned exactly how I had contracted this disease. I then recalled one girl who I smoked with once briefly saying that maybe I should see a doctor. I thought she was kidding since I literally felt alright. Actually what I soon concluded she was doing was telling me that she had the disease and informing me to go get checked, but, the 'bliss' had me so elated that it sunk to the back of my mind.

Back during slavery there was class of Blacks whose sole purpose was to ensure that the master's plans were followed. That's the level I place Dope Sellers. They pass this devil/crack to their own people only to serve the devil. I can honestly say that I could **NEVER** sell any form of drugs to my people… I smoked everything I had; heck, if I had a crack cookie, I would **SMOKE** a crack cookie!!

I had also become a regular with the Task Force for the Homeless Office. These folks have hearts of Gold, and meager resources to do such a powerful task. Eventually I became the **'Homeless Representative' on the Task Force Board of Directors.** The Director of the Task Force was this tiny Lady who had the courage of a Lion!! I started calling her, "Fearless Leader"(circa. Bullwinkle- Rocky the Flying Squirrel) I really enjoyed this feeling of 'prominence'! I attempted to tackle some of the more important problems my fellow homeless folk encountered. **Mouthwash!** This cheap, alcohol-packed liquid was being seriously abused by homeless men and women. My first encounter with mouthwash occurred when this guy I befriended at the Joe House became violently ill one night. 'Big Teddy' became so ill that we were forced to call 911. When the Emergency Medical Technicians, EMTs, arrived, they quickly surmised that the cause of his illness was mouthwash misuse. They told me that mouthwash abuse was rampant in Columbus, Georgia. And, homeless persons would call 911 when they drink too much which further complicates the system since ambulance rides were $750.00.

As a board member of the Task Force for the Homeless, I saw this as a plight to be dealt with. ….so I thought!! I felt compelled to do what I could to stop this abuse, and I figured that my position on the board was the **RIGHT** platform! The media would sugar-coat this dire state when they reported on it instead of viewing the prevailing dangerous condition as what it was and dealing with it promptly. They gave the abusers quaint, cozy, sweet nicknames like, '*Mouthwash Mafia*'; maybe this eased the process to disregard the helpless. Local stores **KNEW** that mouth was being abused, and, they **KNEW** exactly who was abusing mouthwash. They simply made access easier by keeping several cases of cheap mouthwash stacked by the front door. Evidently, since it was being abused primarily by 'pariahs', this made the problem easily overlooked. A large bottle of cheap mouthwash cost $1.00. What makes it truly appealing is the **HIGH** alcohol content, 28.9%. A comparable bottle of name-brand wine, which is sold only at specified sites, liquor stores, may cost $4.99, and only have 18% alcohol. Heck, BoBo the Klown can figure out the best buy!!!

ALL cheap mouthwash contains POISON!! Methyl Salicylate. In large quantities Methyl Salicylate is used by Agriculture as an insecticide. The Food and Drug Administration, FDA, decided that minute amounts may be used in certain products such as mouthwash, as long as 'proper' instructions are there to discourage drinking. Our government has very stringent rules concerning the use of products with more than 5% Methyl Salicyclate since it is known that at over 5% toddlers are directly susceptible to poisoning through ingestion. Little, if anything, is known about the retention capabilities of adults, and, the easily disregarded 'warning labels' on the bottles has about as much bite as a toothless man eating a steak!!! Heck, maybe during times of hopelessness, the aftertaste of mouthwash can be comparable to 101 Proof Jim Beam Whiskey.

Anyway, abuse quickly causes the victim to suffer nerve damage, his/her equilibrium is damaged; the victim also becomes incontinent. Personally, I feel the damages are permanent. Earlier I had contacted the Columbus Police Department, the Columbus Business Improvement District, B.I.D., with negative responses. I was outright offended when a local television station attempted to get me to wear a 'button camera' to document the abuse. I then decided to widen my appeal. I e-mailed the Chief Executive Officer, CEO, of Swan Chemical Company, the largest manufacturer of cheap mouthwashes. To my amazement, within one hour I received a response. Swan's Quality Control Officer informed me that Swan is aware of the abuse, but when they balance that against the profit sheet, they see where it is a top seller in urban areas.

A store chain may order a product at a specific price, and, to be able to remain at that price, cheap alcohol is used. Actually, what I concluded from their response was that the fact that nobody would care if another vagrant was found dead in the street or any vacant house… that's just one less beggar on the streets. This was a blatant example of the ugly, widely used exploitation of the impoverished. What is so ignored is the truth that **Homelessness can happen to ANYONE!'**

I believe that GOD has a Supreme Way of using **EQUALIZERS**!! If you recall any of those horrific disasters we encounter; hurricanes, tornadoes, floods, wildfires, tsunamis, and earthquakes, to name a few. I'm positive that the day before Hurricane Katrina or the last Tsunami there were many of the 'elite' who had such acquired, finicky tastes where only one name-brand item would suffice; coffee, juice, sodas, bread, meat, etc. Three days **FOLLOWING** the disaster, **AFTER** we witnessed the MAJESTY OF GOD, those same folk were hungrily grasping for anything that was **HANDED** to them **Truly** humbling…

Homeless can happen to anyone. There are soooo many causes; you might had barely survived one of **GOD's** 'equalizers', you might have been fired at the wrong time in Life, there might have been tremendous tragedy, you might had been part of downsizing, you might have had debilitating physical/mental conditions, you might had done something downright stupid, or you just might had been wrongfully persecuted, and there was no way to prove your innocence. Those are just a few of the many, many reasons how the state of homelessness will impinge on an existence.

Then it boils down to just how the individual person deals with the situation. Almost daily we read about an irate worker who was fired goes back to the workplace and creates deadly havoc. That is one end of the continuum. The other end may very well be homelessness. Different folk deal with failure in different ways. When confronted with failure some may grab a gun, some may crawl in a bottle, some grab the devil's pipe or needle; anything to somehow soften the painful, degrading feeling of humiliation. Then again, some just open a Bible. I liken homelessness to a natural disaster, perhaps a tornado. Imagine you are on established **SOLID** ground, all indications are that your Life is progressing solidly upward with a limitless forecast when unknown to you everything starts to quiver violently around you. The spiral is so cruel; you lost your job, your family, bank accounts, home, car, etc. With that, added problems/aftershocks begin to arise since there are no funds to pay debtors or rent; no money for food. The spin gets so violent, you are sooo dizzy that when it **DOES** stop spinning, or just slows down a bit, after you had been through sooooo much, that you actually begin to feel a form of contentment.

That just maybe where the trap lies; you see, <u>**'Misery Loves Company'**</u>, and, there are many who have had many different type problems, but if you become destitute and happen to be in a Soup Line where a seasoned homeless person is, he/she, since they may have become somewhat 'comfortable' with their predicament, and seeing you as a novice, will work to convince you to relax, since all **HOPE** is gone, while steadily conniving to convince you to part with your meager resources since you are now part of the downtrodden. An eye-opener for me was witnessing just how devastating devil/crack attacks a female. Women deal with homelessness in ways the average man cannot. Exactly how long those 'skills' may last is dependent on the individual female. I am talking about sisters, Mothers or Grandmothers!! I recall during my school days in Charleston how we would kid each other about what we saw their Mother or Grandmother was doing. Nowadays children risk being ridiculed about what their female kinfolk was actually seen doing…

Another sore point for me was to see those half-wit supposed edumacated students at the local college attempt to imitate homelessness. <u>**You can never imitate homelessness!!**</u> And they had the audacity to camp out on the school's front steps, directly across from the largest **"Burger King"** in the city. First, you can never be homeless if you know that you have a date when this charade is going to end. <u>**PERIOD!!**</u> Sure, you can 'act' like you have nothing, 'play' as if you are destitute, maybe every once in awhile you'll laugh at some hobo jokes; but, deep in the recesses of your mind, you probably thank **GOD** that pretty soon this will be finished and you will be back in your warm comfortable bed!! It is only when lavishness of **ANYTHING** is a lonely nighttime fantasy that you feel hopelessness, when you become susceptible to doing things you never **EVER** imagined, when your best friend is darkness; **THEN AND ONLY THEN ARE YOU HOMELESS!!!**

VI. Dealing wid da Devil

Crack IS the devil!! His weapon, his friend; **crack IS the devil!!** Anything that will make you feel sooooo good, taking you to places you ain't never even dreamed about while literally destroying you, ain't nothing but the devil. Crack will make you do **anything** to get more crack /rock, and all this while you are rapidly becoming a slave; a slave to the devil. And trust me, crack will take **everything** you have. Crack will turn a man into a woman. Crack will make a woman forsake her husband, abandon her child, turn her into the worst whore; while making the person feel soooo damn good! You feel sooo good that you fail to realize just how worthless the substance is making you, or how fast it is doing it.

Crack is the Devil! I was first introduced to Crack by a Black female who was married to a White guy who was unemployed. I met her one day while I was picking up my unemployment check from the employment office. She asked me to give her a ride to her house. Anyway, to get more crack, addicts will entice someone who has money to indulge in a unique experience, unlike any other, while all the time knowing that the person will undoubtedly become another addict; another addict, more crack… ***And believe me, this is exactattackedly the way that devil/crack assaults you! Crack is like 'Lays' potato chips, "you can't take just one."*** This alluring Black female saw that I was alone; then she commenced to light a innocent-looking substance atop a soda can with cigarette ashes. She invited me to try it. As any gullible man would do, I became susceptible because I wanted sex. When she discovered that the effects of crack heightened my sexual skills and learned that I received a unemployment check, she made it a point to invite me to her house daily. The lure was at first she would have a minuscule piece of crack. After awhile I would start giving her money to purchase crack to bring for our rendezvous. Soon after that, if I was with a female, I would start to smoke with at least a fifty dollar piece. At times she would even bring her two babies, then her female friends.

Crack makes a person do some ugly, revolting things. I never knew where my wife was living… I ended up at the 'House of Mercy', a facility for men, women, and families. I lasted only three days there. We slept approximately ten to a room, and, my snoring rapidly made me an undesirable guest.(Now, nobody there had a job to wake up for, but my snoring was unwanted.) I next went back to the Salvation Army. Everybody in the dormitory, 52 men, smoked crack!! At night, you could not get into the bathroom for folk smoking rock. By this time, I was spending my entire $800.00 check on crack. This made me the most popular guy in the neighborhood. I also had my first experience with jail. Being addicted to crack made sleep a distant memory. Yet, after awhile the human body begins to crave rest.

Since my money went to support my habit, I had little pocket change, but, I needed to get something to make me sleep. So, I decided to utilize my questionable skills to acquire/steal sleeping pills. I went into **'Goolsbys'**, a locally-owned grocery chain located within the neighborhood. When you are addicted to crack you have tunnel vision. This vision means that you are completely focused only on what/where your mindset is directed. Consequently, while I placed pills into my pockets I failed to see the store detective who was watching me. He approached me in the parking lot and I broke away and attempted to run. As I said, I was a horrible thief. This was also an 'Obstruction of Justice Charge!! Taken to jail is one humiliating journey. Sitting in jail among other persons accused of crime allowed me to visualize the destructive state that I had placed myself. So, when I appeared before the adjudicator/judge, I pleaded Not Guilty. I was unable to fully express what occurred in my Life which would have had me attended to at a VA hospital. Remember, my diagnosis is **Organic Brain Syndrome**. For me to wait until I was thirty-eight years old before I went to jail is evidence that I have serious issues directly related to OBS. A plea of Not Guilty meant that the case would then be forwarded to State Superior Court for trial. At first I looked forward to this since I lopsidedly figured that the judge would see I needed help and direct me toward treatment. I could not have been more wrong. Judge Allen saw me as another criminal appearing before him and sentenced me accordingly. I was placed on probation.

After seven months, my Mother became severely ill in Charleston. I went to the Probation Office to get permission to travel to see my Mother. Travel was approved. When I got to Charleston, my Mother was in worse condition that I had surmised, so I wrote another letter to my Probation Officer in Columbus, Georgia requesting that my case be transferred. After three months, with no response, I ignorantly mis-figured that my Probation Officer dropped the case since she was originally from Charleston, and her older brother was in my high school homeroom class. Back then he and I were not close, but now that I have his sister for my Probation Officer, He might as well have been one of my BEST friends! I went on with my Life. In between providing 'care' to my Mother, I still struggled with that devil addiction that tended to consume my entire being. I loved that devil so much I chose that over being the son I should have been during my Mother's last days on this earth. I truly, truly, truly regret that. Being an addict blinded me to everything outside of getting more crack. By now I was spending nearly everything I had on crack. I started to sell/pawn valuable objects to get funds for dope. Devil/Crack will **MAKE** you do that! You will sell **ANYTHING** for little or nothing just to get a tiny piece of devil/crack.

When you pawn something, you settle for any small amount, and then you **NEVER** return to pay the debt. I became proficient with selling, but very ignorant on negotiating a proper price. I just needed to get enough to but me a good **'Blast'**. And, like 'Lays' potato chips, I had to get another… My Mother started to improve health-wise. My CDL permit had to be renewed every year. I went to the Motor Vehicle License Office in Charleston. The DMV clerk courteously informed me that there was a computer snafu that should be cleared up within twenty minutes. HAH!!! Within twenty minutes a uniformed policeman rode up and handcuffed me right on the spot. Sooooo embarrassing. I was charged with probation violation. I slept on the floor on a pallet beside the stainless steel toilet for twenty-eight days before I had the chance to appear before Judge John Allen. **GOD** bless Judge Allen. He would let you talk, and he would listen to you if you had intelligent dialogue. Suddenly, a clerk rushed up to the Judge and whispered something to him. He hastily got up and went out the door he used to enter. We later learned that there was a bomb scare at the Government Center. I distinctly thought that we would be escorted back to City Jail; however, they took us back to the lockup on the fourth floor where we PRAYED that the bomb scare was a farce. About one hour later, we were back in court. I had definitely decided that I **HAD** to do something better than this!!!

When I appeared before Judge Allen, my Probation Officer, from the same hometown, emphatically told the judge that she recommended that I be sent to the Diversion Center. When it was my turn to speak, I eloquently spoke to the judge about my upbringing and what transpired to cause me to be in his presence. Evidently, I impressed him because he dismissed my case and as the Guard escorted us back to the Detention Cell he commented that he felt that if the Judge had allowed me fifteen more minutes, I would have had **EVERYONE'S** charges dismissed. (Thank You **GOD** for my Mama inspiring me to be able to verbalize in times of stress) I felt so Blessed when I left that jail!! Yet, each and every day now I get up with the realization that I am a marked **FELON**. This did not stop me from being assigned to jury duty three (3) times, once even chosen to be Jury Foreman!

VII. Discrimination

During early June 2003, the Veteran's Representative at the Georgia Department of Labor directed me to a 'temporary' position as Cemetery Caretaker at Fort Mitchell National Cemetery in Fort Mitchell, Alabama. I was informed that while there was no guarantee, the possibility existed to have the position converted to permanent. The actual hiring was done through an office in Augusta, Georgia. The job started on 14Jul03. One temporary worker was hired with me. We traveled to Decatur, Georgia on 16Jul03 for 'orientation'. Actually, this was only for the purpose of getting our pay properly started.

The Director did not allow us to 'physically' complete the three day orientation.

Even though I jokingly remarked about completing orientation on the ride back, neither of us wanted to question this because we did not want to start off on the wrong foot…When we returned, during the initial daily briefing o/a 17Jul03 was the first time that the Director stated that if ever there was a problem with the temps, he would first side with the permanent employee(s). This was the first of several 'peculiar' statements that the Director made on a regular basis. Because I have 12 years experience as a Non-Commissioned Officer, two as an instructor with the Field Artillery School, two as assistant Inspector General, and, three as Patient Administration NCO at a large army hospital, I figured that my 'people skills' would allow me to get along with anyone. **When the Director made those comments, I feel that he 'paved' the way for the "hostile work environment" that existed during my employment.** We were hired to align all the 240 pound granite headstones within the cemetery. My duty position was extended three times. This was attributed to the fact that Georgia Vocational Rehabilitation paid for my taxi fare, daily, until I was able to get stable. I would arrive daily **BEFORE** anyone else! As I am a dedicated professional, I felt that when the position became open, I would apply, since I knew that I was more qualified than any other temporary at the time. While the intimidations I endured were many, I never ever felt that they would have been able to preclude me being selected for the position.

It was only when I discovered that they indeed did prevent me from being hired was when I realized that "retaliatory tactics" were used to somehow dissuade me about employment at the cemetery. The enclosed copies will disclose my efforts.

Attributed to actions beyond my control, I was homeless for several years. I was in a catastrophic accident in 1999 which took my left eye, and this, I feel, was the basis for many of the deplorable acts taken against me during my employment at Fort Mitchell National Cemetery. From the start, a worker by the name of Wally consistently seemed to have anger against me for reasons unknown. Because I was homeless, he would constantly accuse me of stealing. If I took a tool from the tool room, he took it upon himself to see that it was returned. As I am quite older than Wally, this became very troubling. When I encountered problems with Wally, I confided in Mr. Broadnax, Cemetery Supervisor. Mr. Broadnax was also an ordained minister, and, he and I Prayed on several occasions. As Supervisor, he was able to give me tasks away from Wally, but, Wally would constantly leave his work site to harass me. Another memorable, hurtful, incident was when I saw the necessity for glass safety glasses instead of the plastic ones the cemetery used. Cemeteries are comprised of sand, and, sand scratches plastic very easily, and this presented an extreme problem for me with **ONE** eye. During a morning briefing, when I pleaded to get satisfactory safety glasses, Wally roughly stated, "you're not gonna be here long enough to use them!" This made EVERYONE laugh.

One day as Mr. Broadnax was walking through the cemetery, he stepped into an e=uneven headstone hole and fractured his ankle. He was given convalescent leave for several weeks. It then became "OPEN SEASON" on Henry A. Gaillard. When I first landed this job, I felt extreme pride as to serving as a caretaker within one of this great nation's National Shrines. Also, civil service temporary positions have been known to be converted to permanent assignments quite frequently. On 4Nov03, attributed to Wally, the Assistant Supervisor called me into his office, and with the door wide open loudly stated that I had been urinating on the floor in the bathroom on a daily basis. I felt totally insulted by this remark, but, remembering what the Director said during the initial briefing about siding with the permanent employee, I told the assistant supervisor that this was not true and patiently waited until another rainy day to prove that the floor problem was attributed to the rain.

O/a 14Nov03, again attributed to Wally, I was accused of stealing another worker's cigarettes. I discovered that Wally had an acquaintance that he wanted to be hired when the position was opened, and, since I was the more qualified, I was the most threat. I requested an audience with the Director to specifically address this, and the Director just smiled. Once again, the 'Cemetery Director Apprenticeship Program' opened. I was particularly fastidious about this because I truly felt a sense of purpose working within one of America's National Shrines. After I submitted the packet, I later learned that the paperwork was "lost"!

During early January of 04, I was attempting to purchase an automobile, and, the dealer called the cemetery to verify my employment status. Wally learned of this, and, when he got to his home, he <u>AND</u> his wife called the dealer and worked in EARNEST to wreck my purchase. When I learned of this, I confronted Wally. He called me a **'One-Eyed Son-Of-A-Bitch'!** In spite of my fears, I most definitely HAD to report him on o/a 09Jan04. Wally admitted that he called Bill Heard Chevrolet and spoke to the **SAME** salesman I was working with, admitted that he called me a 'One-Eyed Son-Of-A-Bitch', but, since he was permanent and I was temporary, the Director took no action. Not once did he admonish

Wally for the hurtful, belittling, derogatory statements. Empathize! I literally felt that I was about to be discharged for reporting the event!! Soon after, I was told that my position would be terminated on 29Mar04, I lost the automobile.

I perused the Internet daily, and around mid-June 04 when I discovered that the position was open and being filled through Atlanta, I hastened to apply. I even had my counselor at Georgia Vocational Rehabilitation call! I discovered that a WTC hired **AFTER** me was hired. I then decided to complain. I sent a complaint to MSN in Atlanta. I was advised to contact MPSB via e-mail. I even attempted contact with the Secretary of Veteran's Affairs. **I received little if any response.** *(When I would receive a response, it would be at least 4-6 weeks later)* It was only when I was able to contact Ms. Torrain of the EEO office on Fort Benning that I received the proper address. I would like to commend her for her actions. **Throughout the eight(8) months I was employed at Fort Mitchell National Cemetery, I barely managed to survive the severely cruel tactics which were utilized to intimidate me. As a PROUD Viet Nam-era veteran, it seriously disturbs me to have reported a component of the Department of Veteran's Affairs. Yet, I saw it as my DUTY to assist the department with cleansing itself so as to remain one of America's greatest organizations.**

My initial contact with an EO Counselor was 12Jul05, over 100 days after my employment ceased at Fort Mitchell National Cemetery as a Cemetery Caretaker. My claim was accepted because the claims stated met procedural requirements. My untimeliness is directly attributed to the established fact that I was unaware of the time limits, and has attempted to locate the correct address for filing an EEO complaint through multiple sources to include the Secretary of the VA, Inspector General, Merit System Protection Board (MPSPB) and others without success. If resolution was the focus, anyone of those offices should have been able to direct me. Yet, I only received negative responses. The preliminary investigation was unable to show that I had either actual or constructive notice of EEO time limits and procedures. I was not allowed to complete the three (3) day scheduled orientation wherein I would have been correctly briefed. Therefore, the claims were accepted for investigation. While I understood that ignorance of the law is no excuse, this should not have been held against me since there was a concerted effort to not allow me to be properly hired by the Director of Fort Mitchell National Cemetery.

Since I had 'experience' filing lawsuits Pro Se, and even though I was growing increasingly weary, I made the decision to file a discrimination suit against the Department of Veterans Affairs Fort Mitchell National Cemetery. Previously, I received the 'Final Order', which granted me the authority to file a civil complaint against the Department of Veterans Affairs. In view of the fact that there was a time lapse I still felt confident that this transgression was going to be heard. My first stop was the clerk's office which was located in the Federal Court Building. These proficient clerks, while they were not allowed to give me legal advice were very helpful with answering a few well-placed questions. Questions such as where to locate pertinent information regarding my issues or since there were two law libraries, one in the

Government Center and one in the Federal Building, whose law library would be able to provide additional facts.

Sooooooo, on 24 September 2007, I filed the lawsuit Pro Se. I truly felt confident about this case. There are several prominent lawyers attending St. James AME Church. I made it a point to ask questions so as to stay abreast of the ongoing litigation. The free legal office also gave me limited assistance; I guess this was attributed to my diligence and determination. After attending to each and every action surrounding this case, the judge, rather than rule in my favor, assigned this case to Montgomery, Alabama. This prevented an extreme hardship since I had no car to travel to Montgomery. I protested the change in venue/location, to no avail. Actually this only preceded the biased system's nullification of my lawsuit. I was so disgusted I wrote a letter to President Obama on 18 January 2010. Heck, I wrote President Bush, and President Clinton, too. I took great pride that I was able to convey my feelings on the Executive level and not have the Secret Service question my intent. However, all of my correspondence failed to get me what I desired. The real reason I wrote President Obama was I had earlier scraped-up $450.00 for an appeal to the 11th Circuit court in Hotlanta and the court blatantly upheld the lower court's decision without allowing me to speak! And yes, I was truly prepared to testify on my behalf!!

I was severely disappointed when I was not allowed to appear before the bench. There was this white female army officer who was scheduled to deploy to a war zone. In an effort to thwart the orders, she questioned the President's authority by declaring that he was not born in America. The SAME judge in Columbus, Georgia adjudicated her case to be frivolous, yet sent my case to Montgomery where I saw no justice.

VIII. Free At Last

Even before Fort Mitchell cemetery, when I had earlier obtained my CDL permit, I started driving dump trucks to make money; money that ultimately was used to buy devil/crack. Even though I was not completely legal, I was able to land several dump truck jobs because dump trucks were sorely needed, and they did not check my qualifications that closely. I still was able to smoke devil/crack. I became very proficient with the operation of a dump truck. I truly enjoyed working with the pavement crew as they paved/repaved a road! I drove dump trucks off and on for several years with several of the larger projects of Columbus; the Riverwalk, widening of Macon Road, and J.R. Allen Parkway from the start. What scares me today is the recollection that I actually was a heavy crack smoker while I drove a massive 80,000 lb vehicle, with no regard. That's typical of the feelings of 'superiority' that devil/crack gives to a user. I do have one instance that now and then frightfully comes to mind; one morning as I was leaving the Rock Quarry with a load of gravel, I was traveling south down Veterans Parkway close to the Harris County line and I did indeed see the school bus slowing down as if to stop for children. The bus was in the same lane as I and when he stopped, my brakes failed as I was going 45 mph!! I literally STOOD on the brakes as I downshifted and still the massive beast would not slow down! SO, I PASSED THE BUS BY GOING IN THE INCOMING LANE!! I **Thank God** to this day that no traffic was oncoming and that no child had to cross from the opposite side or I most certainly would be in jail right now doing time for vehicular homicide. …I still continued to smoke devil/crack. Another huge project I drove with was the nighttime repaving of Victory Drive. This was done from 1630/4:30 PM until 0500 AM when Fort Benning traffic begins. There would be these massive machines with actual industrial diamonds attached to huge rollers which would scrape up the old pavement. We, the drivers would deposit this for the purpose of recycling at the asphalt plant ten miles away. We would then rinse out the bed of the truck and load new asphalt to take back to the site. As I was a lifelong lover of trucks, I was in hog-heaven.

Then one day my balloon burst. Earlier, I had gotten a dump truck driving job from the Department of Labor. This job was in Cataula, Georgia, did not require a CDL, and was located at a family-run business where landscape products were sold. As normal, I served at my best for three months. One day I was sent to a quarry to pickup a load of pea gravel. These are called pea- gravel simply because they resemble peas except for the color. Anyway, I was travelling back along the interstate and did not realize that the tarpaulin which covered the load so ragged that stray gravel was being launched with the wind, and, they were striking vehicles behind me. Some Lady whose automobile was hit called the Police and I was given a ticket for unsecured load, $150.00. When I went to Recorder's Court and adamantly proclaimed that I had indeed covered the load, it really did not matter… Sooo, from that point on, I made sure to never get another ticket for unsecured load because this implied that the vehicle was loaded haphazardly. One week later, I was sent to Vulcan Rock Quarry to pick up a load of gravel. Excavation of rock produced is done exclusively with dynamite in Rock Quarries. To witness the magnitude of the quarry is mind-blowing; a huge hole in the earth where humongous vehicles 100s of feet down look like matchbox toys. Anyway, I was in back of the quarry getting my load and when the Tractor Loader finished loading me, he left while I attempted to ensure that I would not get another unsecure load ticket. The spring-loaded tarpaulin was stuck, so I got out of the cab and hanged alongside the bed on one leg while shaking the handle to loosen it. Without warning, the handle, an iron bar about twelve inches long sprung loose and came at me with a 'Willie Mays Home-run swing'. It struck me directly on my left eye! The swing was so violent that it just about knocked me unconscious as it took me off the truck. When I landed on my feet is probably what kept me from losing consciousness. I had presence of mind to realize that nobody would find me as I was in the back of a large rock quarry, so I climbed into the cab of the truck and groggily drove the vehicle towards the truck scales where I knew someone was definitely going to be. I then passed out. When I regained consciousness, I was in one of those recently opened emergency care facilities, Acute Care. When the attendants saw my left eye hanging like a thick slug out of my head, they absolutely **'FREAKED"!!** None knew what to do, probably 'cas their minimal training definitely did not include this; so they just took a paper cup out of the dispenser and taped it over the damaged socket to somehow protect the injured eye.

The owner arrived and took me downtown to Georgia Eye Care. They immediately saw that the damaged eye was beyond repair, and that surgery was required to protect me from further damage. The owner wanted to pay for the hospital to just sew the eye shut, **BUT**, my presence of mind allowed me to demand that I get an opinion from a military doctor. This should have been a crystal-clear clue to me, but I was still in shock as to the devastation of what had transpired and paid it no mind. The owner did not have **ANY** insurance on me; no Workman's Compensation or anything. This was why the owner so quickly wanted to pay the hospital to sew my eye shut. I told the doctor to stop and prepare me to go to a military hospital. I was given the choice of Birmingham Veterans Hospital or Hotlanta, Georgia Veterans Hospital for the Enucleation surgery. Enucleation is the removal of the eye orbit and the insertion of a sponge obtained from the sea which serves a shape as the eyeball which gives the appearance of a normal eye when combined with a glass prosthesis.

I chose Atlanta for the operation and I do not regret the choice. I used to travel for treatment three times a month during the first year. I **LOVED** to travel on the bus to Hotlanta. I was such a customer of Greyhound that one morning when Greyhound's 0500 regular bus from Montgomery to Columbus was delayed, the local station, aware that I had a scheduled 0800 doctor's appointment secured a taxicab for me. I had the driver to allow the meter to run all the way. It totaled $175.00 for the trip to the Greyhound station in downtown Hotlanta. I was so, so angry about the details surrounding my loss eyesight and the realization of just how close I was to being killed, that I refused to wear a cover over the eye for one year. I did not even wear glasses. I was the poster boy for homelessness. Losing an eye was the most devastating thing that **EVER** happened to me!! The loss sincerely touched my understanding of my mortality while fully displaying my appreciation of have using a loop-hole in the law to preclude him from complying with the law to have me covered under Worker's Compensation. The law stated that any Small Business with more than three workers **MUST** Workers Compensation. The sly owner had his son-in-law and his wife working on site, but, on paper he did not have his wife listed as a daily worker; hence, no coverage.

Yes, I did seek legal recourse against him because I was nearly **KILLED!!** We had a mediation scheduled across the street from the courthouse in Columbus, and I just knew that this was about to be settled, and I would get a settlement wherein I could go on with my one-eyed Life. But, this owner swore under oath that there was nothing wrong with his truck. The mediator continued the case. This really incensed me since I later learned that this guy lost his left eye exactly the same way that I lost mine!! I left that office outside of my body. I started to think thoughts I'd never imagined I would. I was figuring just how I could travel the forty-three miles to Cataula, Georgia to burn down the double-wide trailer that this guy lived in. As I was thinking, and planning, I walked down 12th Street in front of the United States Post Office and, by the Grace of **GOD**, Reverend Scottie Swinney was exiting the building. I did not know him, but his collar made him highly visible. I approached him and merely stated, Reverend, I feel so, so troubled…. His reply was simply to come to church on Sunday. Well, this was Wednesday, so I went to the Homeless Task Force Office and the founder was this retired Doctor who earlier had befriended me. I told him that I wanted to go to church but I did not have a suit. Two days later on Friday he gave me one of his old suits. The coat was large enough for my broad shoulders, but the excessive use of crack/devil forced me to have to pin the pants to make them somewhat presentable. I will never forget the pleasurable feeling of peace I felt when I entered the service sitting in the rear of the sanctuary. As I was raised in the AME religion, I felt quite at home… **Then, I forgot about Altar Call!** I feared if I attempted to go to the altar, my pants would fall to the floor. …I slipped out of the door.

The next Sunday, when I obtained better clothing, I met Doctor Emma Hunter. I later found out that the young man who would regularly escort Dr. Hunter up the steps moved to another city. Me being one not to question **GOD**, figured **GOD** fixed it so I would meet this fantastic Lady at a time when we both needed Christ. You see, Dr. Hunter's husband used to pastor this church. One Sunday he collapsed and died while in the pulpit. This happened the **ONE** Sunday that Dr. Hunter stayed home. So, it took **God** to call her home to stop Dr. Emma Hunter from attending Saint James African Methodist Episcopal Church every Sunday since!! If Dr. Hunter was on a Ventilator, the Church bus would've had to been modified; **that's how dedicated she was!!** Plus, this served a dual purpose, because I wholeheartedly believed that only **GOD** could rid me of that devil/crack so each Sunday when I would meet her I would use her key; she was a Trustee, to open the doors and walk throughout the church to ensure it was safe, and then I would kneel at the Altar and Pray to **GOD** to rid me of that devil/crack.

Dr. Hunter was one fantastic Lady!! She utilized a walker because she had very limited movement in her legs and she had an extremely artistic style to transgress the twenty-six granite steps into the sanctuary. The first time I went to grab her arm to assist; she quickly refused my hand and just requested that I walk behind her. We walked those steps every Sunday for several years. She would always get there early for Sunday School, so since I knew this was my Blessing, I would always get there before her so she would not have to sit in the parking lot, since the church was directly across the street from the City Jail, and, when convicts get released on Sunday mornings they would have the tendency to see Dr. Hunter sitting in her pretty Gold Cadillac and **KNOW** they got some breakfast money!!! I received quite a few unique blessings at St. James. Not only did **GOD** rid me of that devil/crack, I also was able to 'kick' the cigarette habit. Now, that was a feat!!! It was only done with the utmost of Faith and belief in the Almighty **GOD**. I admit, when I first started the decline to failure I really started to doubt **GOD**. Yet, after being able to survive so many near-death incidents, and, being able to visualize the vast state of human suffering that that exists with the my fellow homeless men/women, I could only feel Blessed. Through all the miseries and loss that I encountered, combined with the revelations and doors that have been opened as a result, I was able to upgrade my second less than honorable discharge to an Honorable Discharge wherein I was able to attend and graduate from Columbus Technical College with a diploma in Management/Supervisory Techniques and have been awarded service-connected disability status. But, it just seems as if Trials & Tribulations are just an essential part of Life. These Trials & Tribulations just continue to be a necessary part of Life.

THE END

www.ingramcontent.com/pod-product-compliance
Ingram Content Group UK Ltd.
Pitfield, Milton Keynes, MK11 3LW, UK
UKHW050415240426
12048UKWH00020B/1517